A GUIDE TO THE COLLECTIONS
ARWEINLYFR I'R CASGLIADAU

Kim Collis MA DAS

West Glamorgan Archive Service
1998

Gwasanaeth Archifau Gorllewin Morgannwg
1998

Published by
West Glamorgan Archive Service
County Hall, Swansea

ISBN 0 9521783 6 2

FOREWORD

It is a pleasure to introduce this volume, the first published guide to the archival collections which are held by the West Glamorgan Archive Service. The volume is the product of many months' work by my colleague, Kim Collis, and I congratulate him on having produced a work of reference which will become an essential research tool for members of the public studying the many aspects of the history of West Glamorgan and the wider world which are reflected in the collections held by our Service.

Mr Collis has acknowledged the support and assistance of his colleagues in the Archive Service. In turn, I would like to acknowledge the support of the members of the West Glamorgan Archives Committee which includes representatives of the two authorities which fund the Service, namely the City and County of Swansea and Neath Port Talbot County Borough Council. The Archives Committee has been constant in its support and encouragement of all aspects of the work of the Archive Service, including its publications programme, and I pay tribute to the committee members for this.

> **Susan Beckley**
> **County Archivist**
> **West Glamorgan**
> **1998**

RHAGAIR

Mae'n bleser cyflwyno'r gyfrol yma, yr arweinlyfr cyntaf i'r casgliadau archifol sydd dan ofal Gwasanaeth Archifau Gorllewin Morgannwg. Ffrwyth misoedd o waith gan fy nghydweithiwr Kim Collis yw'r gyfrol, a llongyfarchaf ef ar ei gamp o gynhyrchu llyfr cyfeiriol fydd yn gymorth amhrisiadwy i aelodau'r cyhoedd wrth iddynt astudio gwahanol agweddau o hanes Gorllewin Morgannwg a'r byd allanol a gyfeirir atynt yng nghasgliadau'n Gwasanaeth.

Mae Mr Collis wedi cydnabod y cymorth a'r gefnogaeth gafodd gan ei gydweithwyr yn y Gwasanaeth Archifau. Yn fy nhro, dymunaf gydnabod cefnogaeth aelodau Pwyllgor Archifau Gorllewin Morgannwg, sy'n cynnwys cynrychiolwyr o'r ddau awdurdod sy'n ariannu'r Gwasanaeth, sef Dinas a Sir Abertawe a Chyngor Bwrdeistref Sirol Castell Nedd Port Talbot. Mae'r Pwyllgor Archifau wedi bod yn gyson yn ei gefnogaeth a'i nawdd yn holl weithgareddau'r Gwasanaeth Archifau gan gynnwys y rhaglen cyhoeddi, a thalaf deyrnged i aelodau'r pwyllgor am hyn.

> **Susan Beckley**
> **Archifydd y Sir**
> **Gorllewin Morgannwg**
> **1998**

Neath Abbey charter, circa 1129 (A/N 1)

CONTENTS

Contents – continued

Donations and Deposits

Other sources

Indexes of persons and places

LIST OF MAPS AND ILLUSTRATIONS

Maps

Illustrations

INTRODUCTION

The history of the collection of archives and manuscripts in West Glamorgan is similar to that of many Welsh counties. Early collectors of records were the National Library of Wales, local antiquarian and learned societies, central public libraries and later the University of Wales.

In the history of the archive collections which are listed below, a landmark date was the foundation of the Glamorgan Record Office in 1939 by the then Glamorgan County Council. Like so many other county record offices across England and Wales, the new Record Office had its origins in the storage of quarter sessions papers and the County Council's own records from its previous fifty years of existence. After the war, the Record Office was to accept several large collections of estate papers from prominent Glamorgan families. The Local Government (Records) Act of 1962 regularised the position of all county councils in this respect in that it allowed them to accept archive collections from the public and to make them available for research.

The western part of Glamorgan has always had a distinct identity from the rest of the historic county, and this was recognised in 1974 by the creation of a separate county of West Glamorgan. The Glamorgan Record Office continued to serve the three new counties of Mid, South and West Glamorgan by means of a joint agreement between the three authorities, and in 1984 opened an Area Record Office in the new County Hall in Swansea. Collections relating to West Glamorgan were transferred to Swansea from Cardiff, the office having been recognised by the Lord Chancellor and the Master of the Rolls as suitable for the storage of public records and tithe and manorial records respectively. Parish records from the southern half of the Diocese of Swansea and Brecon were transferred to Swansea under the 1976 Agreement with the Church in Wales.

In 1992, West Glamorgan County Council withdrew from the tripartite agreement and established an independent County Archive Service. More recently, following the 1996 reorganisation of local government in Wales, the situation has altered again: the West Glamorgan Archive Service is a joint archive service established to serve the two unitary authorities, the City and County of Swansea and the County Borough of Neath Port Talbot, which together comprise the area of the former county of West Glamorgan. In this way, the integrity of county-wide collections has been preserved. At this time, the holdings of the Swansea City Archives Office, which had served the former Swansea City Council since 1974, were combined with the county-wide collections.

Today, the West Glamorgan Archive Service is one of the largest archive services in Wales and plays a vital part in the preservation of the written heritage of West Glamorgan, running two searchrooms in County Hall Swansea, with Archive Access Points in Neath and Port Talbot.

The Archive Service also provides a records management service to both unitary authorities, managing their deeds and other legal documents, and providing expertise in the retention and disposal of records generally. The facilities available in Swansea include archive storage premises to British Standard 5454, a conservation unit and, most importantly, trained professional staff.

It is the object of this guide to bring to the general reader something of the richness of the archives held by the Service. The principal unit of description is the archive collection. This may be loosely defined as a series of records with the same provenance, not necessarily deposited at the same time, which bear some administrative relationship to each other, be it the records of a chapel, a business, or an individual's personal papers. However, many items are listed individually where they are of particular subject interest. The guide is structured by division into public records (records of central government), official records (local government records), ecclesiastical parish records and nonconformist records, then a large section devoted to donated and deposited archives, this being divided into different subject categories including records of landed estates and business records. Final sections look at archive material which is easily classified by type, such as maps, newspapers and photographs. Each entry is followed by an archive reference to the collection from which it comes. Where a collection or particular items have restrictions on access, this is noted at the relevant point: researchers wishing to use such items should write to the County Archivist in advance of their visit, giving details of their research interest. Abbreviations have been avoided in the text as much as possible, the two exceptions being *n.d.* for 'no date' and *mf* for 'microfilm.'

Every effort has been made to make this guide as inclusive as possible, but it is in the nature of things that some errors or omissions may have occurred, for which I offer my apologies. Where a collection is unlisted, it has been entered to indicate that such records exist, but in the majority of cases such records may not be made available to the public until they are listed. Accessions subsequent to the date of publication of this guide are listed in the *Annual Report of the County Archivist*.

This guide could not have been produced without the generosity of the many donors and depositors of the records listed in the following pages. I am grateful to the County Archivist, Miss Susan Beckley, for initiating and supporting this project. I am also grateful to my colleague, Mr Andrew Dulley, for his help in preparing the maps.

Kim Collis
Principal Archivist
1998

PUBLIC RECORDS

PUBLIC RECORDS

Public records are records of central government, its agencies and those nationalised industries which come under the scope of the Public Records Acts of 1958 and 1967.

Section 4(1) of the 1958 Act makes provision for the Lord Chancellor to appoint places of deposit outside the Public Record Office for specified classes of public records. The repository at County Hall Swansea is a recognised local place of deposit for certain central government records relating to the area of the county of West Glamorgan. It is also the recognised repository for NHS records in the area served by the West Glamorgan Health Authority.

The types of public record deposited with the Archive Service include those generated locally, such as petty sessions and coroner's records, and those generated centrally which have local interest, such as the 1910 land valuations.

Under Section 3(6) of the 1958 Act, the Lord Chancellor is empowered to present records not required for permanent preservation by the Public Record Office to local record offices. Some of the records listed below are presentation records from various government departments and, strictly speaking, cease to be public records when presented, but for convenience' sake are listed here.

QUARTER SESSIONS

The court of quarter sessions derives its name from the quarterly meeting of justices of the peace for the county in order to determine legal cases and to carry out essential administrative duties of county government. The latter function was lost with the creation of county councils in 1888.

All original records of the Glamorgan Quarter Sessions are held at the Glamorgan Record Office, Cardiff. The West Glamorgan Archive Service holds records of the County Borough of Swansea Quarter Sessions, 1930-1971. In 1972, Swansea's Court of Quarter Sessions amalgamated with the Assize Court to become Swansea Crown Court.

Restrictions on access: 30-year rule applies to all records below.

Glamorgan Quarter Sessions

Land Tax Assessments: Llangyfelach Hundred, 1772-1831 (with gaps); Neath Hundred, 1784-1831 (with gaps); Swansea Hundred, 1766-1831 (with gaps); Swansea Town, 1766-1831 (with gaps) (mf: LTA/Lf, N, S and SBo); land and window tax assessments for Newcastle Hundred, 1704-1710 (D/D P); transcript and index to Land and Window Tax Assessments for Swansea Town and Franchise, 1788 (D/D Z 164)

Enclosure Awards: Loughor Enclosure Act, 1833 (D/D Z 137) and plan, 1835 (TT/Lw); Townhill Enclosure award (Facsimile Collection) and plan, 1762 (EA)

Plan of Swansea designed for supplying the Town with water from the adjoining hills, 1835 (photograph of Glamorgan Q/DP 54)

Swansea Borough Quarter Sessions

Minutes, 1941-1971; recorder's notebooks, 1891-1924, 1930-1971; sessions files, 1947-1971 (Q/S SBo)

PETTY SESSIONS

The earliest petty sessions records listed below date from the 1840s. The original petty sessions divisions were based on the old hundredal boundaries of Swansea, Neath and Llangyfelach. Borough petty sessions were established later and, subsequently, in 1974 new divisions were created co-terminous with the district councils of Swansea, Lliw Valley, Neath and Port Talbot.

Restrictions on access: 30-year rule applies to most record classes. Records relating to adoptions are closed for 100 years

Aberavon Petty Sessions

Court registers, 1894-1974; register of licences, 1903-1938; register of clubs, 1903-1938; register of fines and fees, 1901-1959; minute books, 1926-1953; information books, 1929-1944 (P/S A)

Gower Petty Sessions

Court registers, 1914-1974; registers of fines and fees, 1941-1955; minute books, 1891-1974; club returns, 1941-1949 (P/S G)

Llangyfelach Petty Sessions

Minute books, 1845-1870 (P/S Lf)

Lliw Valley Petty Sessions

Court registers, 1974-1987; adoption orders, 1974-1983; minutes, 1974-1986; information book, 1974-1981 (P/S Lli)

Neath Borough Petty Sessions

Court registers, 1924-1986; registers of licences, 1894-1962; minute books, 1891-1956; adoption papers, 1925-1950; bastardy papers, 1894-1913; separation and maintenance orders, 1894-1913; licensing files, 1921-1953; justices' lists, 1923-1954; commissions of the peace, 1893-1950 (P/S NBo); commissions of the peace and related papers, 1893-1950 (D/D Z 73)

Neath Hundred Petty Sessions

Court registers, 1933-1973; register of licences, 1903-1931; register of clubs, 1930-1962; register of music and dancing licences, 1930-1955; adoption of children register, 1930-1948; minute books, 1937-1955, 1963-1969 (P/S N)

Pontardawe Petty Sessions

Court registers, 1880-1964; registers of licences, 1903-1969; registers of fines and fees, 1904-1930; minute books, 1870-1974; adoption orders, 1927-1950 (P/S Pd)

Port Talbot Petty Sessions

Court registers, 1919-1990; register of clubs, 1921-1940; registers of licences, 1920-1941, 1978-1985; registers of fines and fees, 1900-1904, 1950-1955; minute books, 1920-1940; Borough Commission, 1953-1954 (P/S PT)

Swansea Borough Petty Sessions

Court registers, 1934-1992; registers of licences, 1881-1962; registers of clubs, 1930-1962; registers of fines and fees, 1947-1979; minute books, 1846-1981; clerk's notebooks, 1954-1968 (P/S SBo)

Swansea, Gower and Pontardawe Petty Sessions

Probation register, 1924-1949 (P/S SG&Pd)

Swansea Hundred Petty Sessions

Court registers, 1880-1974; register of licences, 1903-1967; registers of fines and fees, 1927-1955; registers of clubs, 1903-1939; minute books, 1844-1973; club returns, 1937-1949; information book, 1953-1961 (P/S S)

CORONER'S RECORDS

Coroners were originally royal officers who, from the Middle Ages onwards, held inquests into matters affecting crown rights in the country, including sudden death, treasure trove and wrecks.

Very few of the older records for West Glamorgan have survived. Amongst the Glamorgan Quarter Sessions records at the Glamorgan Record Office, Cardiff there are returns of inquests, 1869-1875: however, the majority of such records are presumed to have been destroyed.

Restrictions on access: 75-year closure applies to all records

West Glamorgan Coroner: Coroner's daily record books, 1921-1933; case papers for inquests held at Neath and Port Talbot, 1960s-1970s (unlisted) (COR/W)

REGISTRY OF SHIPPING

A large collection of public records forms the core of the maritime records held by the Archive Service. These are registers from the Swansea Registry of Shipping, 1824-1954, with crew agreements for ships registered in Port Talbot and Swansea, 1863-1913 (sometimes including ship's logs and associated papers).

Shipping registers: these volumes contain full details of the dimensions, ownership and transactions of ownership, history and ultimate fate of each ship registered in the port, arranged in chronological order of registration, 1824-1897 (D/D PRO/RBS/S).

Transactions registers: these volumes record transfers of ownership and mortgages, 1855-1934. Each volume may contain details of transactions which are of later date than the given covering dates (D/D PRO/RBS/S).

Register of Fishing Boats: this volume contains details of the dimensions, ownership, history, number of crew, name of skipper, mode of fishing, and ultimate fate of each vessel, arranged in chronological order of registration, 1903-1935 (D/D PRO/RBS/S).

Ship's registration papers: These papers give details of the dimensions of each ship, a declaration of ownership and certificate of registration, 1825-1954 (with gaps, partly listed) (D/D PRO/SR/S)

Crew agreements: these documents set the terms and conditions of the voyage, to which each member of the crew had to give his assent. They covered such matters as the length and destination of the voyage, and the minimum rations to be provided. Crew agreements list the names and capacities of the crew members, and details of each one's previous ship. The document was stamped at each port of call during the voyage and was handed in at the end of the voyage when the crew were paid off. The series covers the period 1863-1913 for the ports of Swansea and Port Talbot, Port Talbot documents being interleaved with those of Swansea. The Archive Service lacks agreements for 1861, 1862 and years ending in 5: these are held by the National Maritime Museum at Greenwich. The Public Record Office also retained an overall 10% sample before transfer. Despite this, the collection occupies 240 boxes and provides valuable information on the crews of Swansea and Port Talbot ships. There is an index to ship's masters, but the crew lists have not been indexed by name (D/D PRO/CA/S).

Ship's logs and associated papers: such records sometimes accompany crew agreements and are filed with them (D/D PRO/CA/S).

For other maritime records not classed as public records, see sections below, *South Wales Sea Fisheries Committee* and the general section, *Maritime Records*.

HOSPITAL RECORDS

Records have been collected from a number of hospitals in this area. Of particular note is a fine collection from the now-closed Swansea Hospital. Some of those hospitals which developed from workhouse infirmaries have related records amongst those of the relevant poor law union: these are detailed in the section *Poor Law Unions*. Related records are also to be found in the sections on municipal records.

Restrictions on access: Administrative records are closed for 30 years. Patients' records, and other records which identify individuals, are closed for 100 years.

Ministry of Health

Annual reports, 1931-1939; reports of the Chief Medical Officer, 1920-1937 (D/D PRO/MOH)

West Glamorgan Health Authority and its predecessors

Glamorgan NHS Executive Committee: minutes, 1947-1969 (D/D PRO/NHS)

Glantawe Hospital Management Committee: minutes, 1958-1974; annual reports, 1948-1972; attendance books, 1965-1973; newscuttings, 1969-1974 (D/D H/Gl)

Welsh Board of Health: files relating to the provision of hospitals in the Swansea area, 1957-1969 (D/D WBH)

Welsh Hospital Board: agenda papers, 1965-1972; annual reports, 1951-1973 (D/D WHB); history, 1974 (D/D Z 186)

West Glamorgan Health Authority: minutes, 1974-1988; Area Team minutes and papers, 1974-1982; deeds, 1881-1980; correspondence files (unlisted); papers of J H Button, former General Manager, 1971-1985 (unlisted) (D/D H/WGHA)

Hospitals

Cefn Coed Psychiatric Hospital, Swansea: minutes, 1932-1963; visiting committee agendas, 1932-1948; Medical Advisory Committee papers, 1958-1971; reports and other administrative records, 1932-1970; newscuttings, 1932-1981; printed material, 1932-1982 (D/D H/CC); brochure for opening ceremony, 1932 (D/D Z 64)

Clydach Cottage Hospital: Trustees' Committee minutes, 1922-1948 (D/D H/Cly)

Graig House Maternity Hospital, Swansea: patients' records, 1920-1942 (D/D H/Gra)

Mount Pleasant Hospital, Swansea: patients' records, 1929-1980 (D/D H/MP)

Port Talbot and District General Hospital: annual report, 1947 (D/D H/PT)

Rheanfa House Maternity Hospital, Swansea: patients' records, 1926-1943 (D/D H/Rhe); midwife's register, 1931-1940 (D/D X 192)

Singleton Hospital, Swansea: brochure for opening ceremony, 1968 (D/D Z 64)

Stouthall Hospital, Reynoldston: patients' records, 1942-1954 (D/D H/Sto)

Swansea Hospital: minutes, 1817-1948; annual reports, 1848-1905; accounts, 1862-1948; salaries and wages books, 1913-1945; plans, *circa* 1876; papers relating to legacies and bequests, 1844-1933; miscellaneous items, including letter and photograph from Florence Nightingale, 1865, and application for a position from Edith Cavell, 1901; newscuttings, 1902-1965; staff registers (domestics) 1907-1950; patients' records, 1931-1947 (D/D H/S); historical notes, *circa* 1960 (D/D X 51); miscellaneous photographs and ephemera, 1904-1966 (D177)

General medical practices

Records relating to general medical practices at Cwmllynfell, *circa* 1940-1980 (D/D Z 237)

Letter from Florence Nightingale commenting on plans for a new building for Swansea Hospital, 1865 (D/D H/S 129)

OTHER PUBLIC RECORDS

British Railways Board

Share registers of pre-grouping railway companies. All were absorbed into the Great Western Railway at various dates up to 1923 (D/D PRO/BRB)

Briton Ferry Docks Company: register of probate, 1855-1867

Dulais Valley Mineral Railway Company: proprietors' ledger, share register and register of share transfers, 1862-1892

Neath and Brecon Railway Company: share registers, registers of share transfers and of probate, 1870-1922

Port Talbot Railway and Dock Company: share registers, share conversion registers, registers of share transfers and of probate, 1895-1922

Rhondda and Swansea Railway Bay Company: share registers, share conversion registers, registers of share transfers and of probate, 1890-1922

South Wales Mineral Railway Company: share registers, 1900-1921

Swansea Harbour Trust: share registers and share conversion registers, 1921-1923

Vale of Neath Railway: share conversion register and register of probate, 1847-1870 (includes address on the opening of the Vale of Neath Railway, 1863)

Charity Commission

Accounts of charities in the West Glamorgan area, 1900-1954 (D/D PRO/Ch)

Central Land Board

The Central Land Board was established in 1947 to levy charges on new developments and to compensate other landowners for loss of development value because of planning restrictions. The files relate to claims for compensation in the West Glamorgan area, 1948-1955 (D/D PRO/CLB)

Department of Education

Architectural plans of primary schools, *circa* 1840-1892, submitted to central government for educational building grants, including the following: Aberavon National; Briton Ferry National; Bryncoch National; Cadoxton National; Cheriton, Llanmadoc and Llangennith National; Clydach National; Crynant National; Llandeilo Talybont National; Loughor National; Morriston British; Neath Alderman Davies Charity; Neath School Society British;

Neath Abbey British; Neath Abbey National; Neath Higher National; Neath Higher National; Penclawdd National; Pontardawe; Swansea National; Swansea Goat Street British; Swansea Queen Street British Girls; Swansea St David's Roman Catholic; Swansea St Peter's National (D/D PRO/EBG)

Health and Safety Executive

Plans of abandoned collieries in West Glamorgan, 1857-1962, including: Aberbaiden, Abergelli, Aberpergwm, Broadoak, Bryn Lliw, Caeduke, Cefn-y-bryn, Clydach Merthyr, Courtherbert, Cwmgwrach, Elba, Garn Goch, Garth, Geli Wern, Glyn Castle, Glyn Cymmer, Glynneath, Gorseinon, Graig Merthyr, Grovesend, Guerets, Gwaun Cae Gurwen, Killan, Kilvey Mount, Llangyfelach, Moodys Graigola, Morlais, Mountain, Mynydd y Caerau, Mynydd Newydd, Oakland, Oakwood, Ogmore Vale, Onllwyn, Parc-y-bryn, Penallta, Penclawdd, Seven Sisters, Tirdonkin, Ton Hir and Ynispenllwch Graigola Collieries (D/D PRO/HSE)

Inland Revenue

Land valuation books prepared under the Finance Act 1910, giving details of landowners and occupiers in West Glamorgan (Swansea, Port Talbot and part of the Llanelli Assessment areas), 1909-1910; provisional valuation forms for the Swansea Assessment Area (Forms 37), 1911-1916 (D/D PRO/VAL)

National Coal Board

Plans of colliery waste tips, 1975-1987, including Aberpergwm, Blaengwrach, Cefn Coed, Hendy Merthyr and Margam

Plans of colliery pit-head buildings, 1931-1984, including Abercrave, Abernant, Aberpergwm, Bryn, Brynlliw, Cwmgorse, Cwmgwrach, Dare, Felin Fran, Garth Tonmawr, Glyncastle, Glyncorrwg, Gwaun Cae Gurwen East Pit, Maerdy and Steer Pits, Onllwyn, Tirbach, Treforgan

Plans of the South Wales Coalfield, 1957-1960

Colliery accident books for West Glamorgan collieries, *circa* 1920-1950 (unlisted) (D/D PRO/NCB)

Vehicle licensing records

Borough of Swansea: registers of vehicle licences for motor cars and motor cycles, 1920s, including numbers CY1-5435; registers of trade plates, 1932-1959, including numbers 145-498CY; registers of driving licences, 1904-1930; offence report books, 1921-1966 (D/D PRO/VL/S)

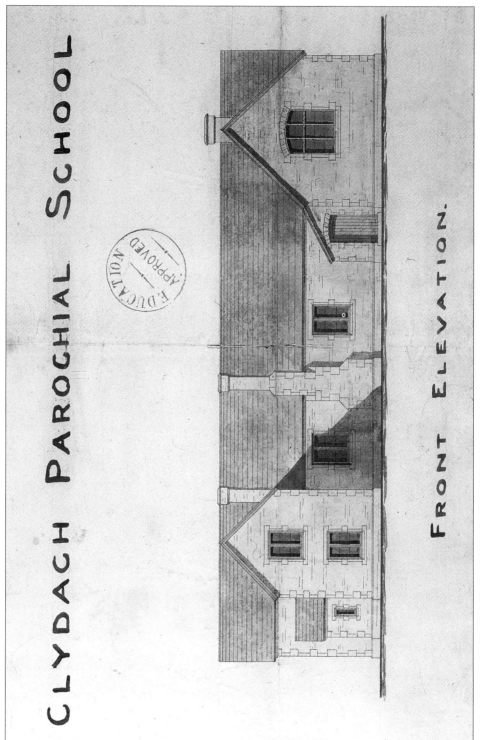

Architect's plan for Clydach National School, 1862 (D/D PRO/EBG 24)

OFFICIAL RECORDS

OFFICIAL RECORDS

Official records here are records created by the two authorities, the City and County of Swansea and the County Borough of Neath Port Talbot, which in 1996 established and today run the West Glamorgan Archive Service, together with the records of all their predecessor authorities. These range from borough and county councils to highway boards and local boards of health.

The Local Government Act 1972 required all principal councils to make proper arrangements for the care of any documents which belong to them or are in their custody. This was reinforced by the Local Government (Wales) Act 1994, which under Section 60 required all principal councils to make and maintain schemes for the care, preservation and management of their records. The West Glamorgan Archive Service manages current administrative records from both its constituent authorities and accepts from them on deposit records considered worthy of permanent preservation.

The principal arrangement of the section below is loosely hierarchical, based on the size and status of the authority. Education records are treated separately, since this is a large subject. Also included in this section are records of the South Wales Police Authority and the South Wales Sea Fisheries Committee.

LIEUTENANCY

The office of lord lieutenant was a Tudor creation. The lord lieutenant was, and remains, the sovereign's representative in each shire. Today, the lords lieutenant in Wales continue to serve the 'preserved' counties of Wales, that is the pre-1996 counties (as do the high sheriffs).

Appointment of John, Earl of Bridgwater as Lieutenant for Wales, Monmouthshire, Herefordshire, Worcestershire and Shropshire, 1631; appointment of Henry, Marquis of Worcester as Lieutenant for North and South Wales, 1672; appointments of Deputy Lieutenants, 1674-1796 (D/D RE)

Grant of arms to Thomas William Booker, Deputy Lieutenant of the Counties of Hereford and Glamorgan, 1855 (Lieut 3)

Correspondence addressed to Christopher Rice Mansel Talbot, Lord Lieutenant of Glamorgan, 1889 (D/D Ma)

County Clerk's file on the Lieutenancy, 1975-1976 (*closed for 30 years*) (D/D X 46)

SHRIEVALTY

The office of sheriff is the oldest surviving secular office in the land, having its origins in Anglo-Saxon society. In the early modern period, the majority of the sheriff's powers passed to the justices of the peace and the lords lieutenant. Nowadays it is primarily a ceremonial post, with the much of the surviving judicial work carried out by the under-sheriff. The high sheriff holds office for a year.

List of Sheriffs of the County of Glamorgan, 1541-1763 (D/D RE)

Warrants of appointment and declarations of High Sheriffs of West Glamorgan, 1986-date (HS/W)

COUNTY COUNCILS

Until the late nineteenth century, the administrative work of counties was carried out by justices of the peace acting in quarter sessions. The Local Government Act 1888 created county councils to take over this growing administrative activity. The largest towns and cities were excluded from county government and made autonomous county boroughs.

Glamorgan County Council was created in 1888. In 1889, Swansea was made a county borough. County councils took on new powers and responsibilities under subsequent legislation, notably the Education Act 1902 and the Local Government Act 1929.

Glamorgan County Council was abolished in 1974 and its powers transferred to three successor counties, Mid, South and West Glamorgan.

The bulk of Glamorgan County Council records are at the Glamorgan Record Office, Cardiff. However, the West Glamorgan Archive Service holds some Glamorgan County Council records of local significance, such as education records and those of public assistance institutions. These are described below in the sections *School Boards and Local Education Authorities*, *School Records* and *Poor Law Unions*.

The main series of county council records held by the Archive Service is that of West Glamorgan County Council, which existed from 1974 to 1996. Pre-1974 records are also to be found in this series, since they were used by West Glamorgan County Council for administrative purposes.

Restrictions on access: 30-year rule applies to most record classes.

Glamorgan County Council

Minutes, 1923-1974; year books, 1892-1974 (GCC/C); estimates of income and expenditure, 1931-1967; abstracts of accounts, 1960-1973; summaries of accounts, 1942-1973 (GCC/FIN)

West Glamorgan County Council

Grant of arms, 1975

Chief Executive's Department: annual reports, 1980-1994; publications, 1989-1993; Economic Development Unit publications, 1983-1995 (WGCC/CE)

County Secretary's Department: correspondence, 1974-1996; minutes and committee papers, 1974-1996 (WGCC/CS)

Education Department: West Glamorgan schools grouping statistics, 1962-1987 (WGCC/Ed). See also *School Boards and Local Education Authorities* and *School Records*.

Environment and Highways Department: correspondence, 1981-1990 (mf); publications, 1974-1987; photographs, 1974-1996; planning applications, 1953-1982 (mf); road improvement plans, 1926-1976; measured drawings of listed buildings, 1976-1985; Margam Country Park miscellanea, 1982-1986 (WGCC/EH, WGCC/Pl/X)

Finance Department: financial abstracts, 1974-1980 (WGCC/FIN)

Property Services Department: terrier of Glamorgan County Council properties in West Glamorgan, 1950s; school plans, 1908-1939; plans showing air raid damage in Swansea, 1941 (WGCC/PS)

Social Services Department: plans of social services premises, 1940-1985; Gelligron Home for the Aged, registers of residents, 1953-1976 (*closed for 100 years*) (WGCC/SS)

Trading Standards Department: annual reports, 1983-1995 (WGCC/CP)

BOROUGHS

There were four medieval boroughs in the area of West Glamorgan- Loughor, Swansea, Neath and Aberavon. Medieval boroughs were established by a charter, or series of charters, which granted a measure of self-government, and trading rights such as the rights to hold a market and a fair.

Borough government was reformed under the Municipal Corporations Act 1835, with the provision of elected councils and improved financial regulation. During the nineteenth century, further powers were given to boroughs in fields such as public health and policing.

Following the Local Government Act 1888, county boroughs were created in towns of 50,000 population or more. County boroughs were completely autonomous from the surrounding county and in 1889 Swansea was made one. In 1969, by royal prerogative, it was granted city status.

The Borough of Aberavon merged with Margam Urban District Council in 1921 to form the Borough of Port Talbot.

Boroughs and county boroughs ceased to exist in 1974, becoming district councils. However, under the provisions of the Local Government Act 1972, conurbations were able to petition for borough status and the new district councils of Lliw Valley, Neath and Afan (Port Talbot) all became boroughs. Swansea retained the title of City. See *District Councils 1974-1996* for borough and city records of later date.

Aberavon charter, circa 1307 (B/A 1)

Borough of Aberavon (from 1921, Port Talbot)

Pre-1835 records: charter, *circa* 1307; ordinances as to the letting of Corporation lands, 1651; register of burgesses' lands, 1788 (B/A); plan of borough with ruling on boundaries by Parliamentary commissioners, *circa* 1831 (D/D Xlm)

Records 1835-1974: case against and opinion as to creating a new municipal corporation, 1859; papers concerning the legality of the 1861 charter, 1861-1863; deeds, 1848-1938; Town Clerk's incoming correspondence, 1894-1910; burgess roll, 1861-1882; poll book, 1867-1870; minutes, 1861-1974; borough plan with proposed extension, 1899; bye-laws, 1906; committee reports and related material, 1937-1955; registers of mortgages, 1867-1952; ledger, 1914-1917; General Rate Fund ledgers, 1926-1954, and other account books, 1921-1960; rating records, 1924-1966 (B/A, B/PT, PTL B/A and PTL B/PT)

Fairfield housing scheme plan, 1919; miscellaneous Surveyor's records, 1952-1962; slum clearance plans, 1930-1938 (PTL B/A and PTL B/PT); planning applications and plans for domestic and industrial premises, 1923-1959 (PTL B/PT Pl)

Market Inspector's report books, 1902-1936; accounts of tolls received on the market, beach and promenade, 1903-1956; record of civilian war deaths, 1940-1941; civil defence records, 1938-1942; burial records, 1932-1961; cemetery records, 1952-1962; cemetery plans, n.d.; registers of factories, 1938-1964; petroleum and other licences, 1948-1961 (B/PT and PTL B/PT); records relating to Aberavon market, 1855-1859 (D/D Xk); miscellaneous minor legal agreements, 1922-1972 (D/D Z 25)

Borough of Loughor

Corporation minutes, 1833-1873; applications to fill alderman vacancies, 1876-1881; applications to buy or rent Corporation land, 1874-1880; burgess lists, 1868-1874; accounts, 1871-1881; correspondence, 1867-1880; plans, 1835-1875; Loughor Town Trust minutes, 1890-1928 (TT/Lw)

See also *Swansea Rural District Council* in the following section, *Urban and Rural District Councils and Local Boards of Health.*

Borough of Neath

Pre-1835 records: copies of Borough charters, 1396-1423; Corporation minutes, 1819-1834; Town Hall Committee minutes, 1819-1922; Court of Pleas minutes, 1759-1780, 1806-1818; Court Baron and Court Leet minutes, 1741-1823; register of deeds, 17th-18th centuries; deeds, 18th-19th centuries (B/N); map of boundaries, *circa* 1832 (D/D X 34)

Records 1835-1974: minutes, 1835-1971; committee minutes, 1871-1968 (B/N and NL B/N); Urban Sanitary Authority minutes, 1872-1894; Urban District Council minutes, 1894-1921 (B/N); Profiteering Committee minutes, 1919; councillors' declaration books, 1835-1910; poll record books, 1881-1933; register of mortgages, 1887-1920; bye-laws 1870s-1900s; Neath Gas Act, 1866; Gas Inspector's minute book, 1869-1886; Highway Board minutes, 1876-1880; Neath Joint Hospital Committee minutes, 1912-1939; Neath and District Tramways Company Ltd minutes, 1876-1885; Neath Local Benefit Society and Savings Band minutes, 1857-1885; Neath, Swansea and Aberavon Borough extension inquiry, 1920-1922; Neath Constabulary, correspondence (unlisted); Neath Education Board, correspondence (unlisted); correspondence on markets, public health and Neath Harbour (unlisted) (NL B/N); accounts, 1924-1972; rating records, 1876-1968 (NM B/N)

Register of new dwellings, 1957-1962 (NM B/N); Medical Officer of Health records, 1918-1974; Public Health Inspector records, 1933-1972, including overcrowding survey of 1936 and records of children evacuated to Neath, 1940-1945; statutory registers, 1851-1963; Weights and Measures Department records, 1890-1960 (B/N) Other records (B/N, partly listed); records of the 4th Glamorgan (Neath) Battalion Home Guard, 1940-1944 (D/D Z 326)

Borough of Port Talbot see *Borough of Aberavon* above

Borough of Swansea (from 1889 County Borough, from 1969 City)

Pre-1835 records

Notice restricting sale of farm produce to the new market, 1815 (D/D Xgb); Acts of Parliament relating to Swansea, 1791-1822 (D/D Xjk)

The Library of the University of Wales, Swansea holds Borough charters, 1234-1836; Common Hall books and Council minute books, 1547-1852; financial and estate records, 1617-1857; and Town Clerk's office papers, 1830-1902. See section below *Related Records in other Repositories.*

Records 1835-1889

Minutes, 1852-1889; committee minutes, 1847-1880; burgess rolls, 1839-1889 (TC); rate books, 1845-1889; accounts, 1854-1889 (TR)

Swansea Paving and Lighting Commissioners: minutes, 1842-1850; Surveyor's day book, 1845-1848; contract book, 1844 (TC 66)

Swansea Local Board of Health: minutes, 1850-1879; registers of mortgages, 1851-1877; correspondence, 1855-1882; Surveyor's report books, 1860-1882; water works report books, 1855-1870; Sanitary Inspector's report books, 1857-1863, 1866-1870; registers of licences for hackney carriages, 1864-1872; registers of slaughter houses, 1853-1870; register of lodging houses, 1851-1853 (TC 67); accounts, 1851-1894; rate books, 1880-1890 (L/B S)

Swansea Urban Sanitary Authority: annual reports of the Medical Officer of Health, 1874-

1889 (series continues, see below under *Health*) (HE); records relating to the Borough of Swansea Improvement Scheme 1876, 1873-1880 (TC 67); rate books, 1881-1907; accounts, 1872-1912 (TR)

Records 1889-1974

Town Clerk: Grant of arms, 1922; grant of city status, 1969; town twinning agreements, 1978-1992

(Lord) Mayor's correspondence and engagement files, 1913-1974; visitors' books, 1920-1974; diaries, 1960-1974; hereditary freemen's rolls, 1780 onwards; honorary freemen's roll, 1887-1960 (TC)

Minutes, 1889-1974; committee minutes, 1889-1974; bye-laws, various dates; seal registers, 1956-1974; contracts, *circa* 1920-1950; yearbooks, 1882-1974; correspondence, 1895-1969; correspondence with central government, 1872-1934; local Acts, 1762-1986; bye-laws, 1853-1977; papers concerning legal case, Graigola Merthyr Company Ltd *vs* Swansea Corporation, 1926-1927; electoral registers, 1889-1974, and other election material (TC)

Swansea Battalion Committee records (including records of the Swansea Belgian Refugees Committee), 1914-1930; records of the Prince of Wales' National Relief Fund, 1914-1925 (TC)

Grand Theatre records, including correspondence, programmes and posters, 1898-1974 (series continues, see *District Councils 1974-1996*)(TC); Glyn Vivian Art Gallery records (unlisted) (LE); records of the Director of Music, including concert programmes and files, 1934-1981 (TC and LE)

Air Raid Precautions (and related non-Council material): requisition of property files, 1940-1956 (TC 200); list of air raid deaths, 1940-1943 (D32); documents relating to ARP in Swansea, 1940-1943 (D42); documents relating to the Fire Service, *circa* 1940-1945 (D68); plan of Fairwood Common aerodrome, 1945 (D38); diary of 103 Bomb Disposal Station, Royal Engineers, 1940-1941 (D258); diary of air raid warden in Swansea, 1940-1941 (D/D Z 126); diary of civilian in Swansea, *circa* 1940-1945 (D35, *restricted access*: only by prior written permission from the County Archivist); transcript of ARP Controller's statement to Council concerning the Three Nights' Blitz, 1941 (D125)

Architect: plans and files relating to the Guildhall, 1930-1947; site plans of school premises destroyed or damaged in air raids, 1939-1945; environmental design papers relating to parks and landscaping, 1928-1974 (BA)

Education: minutes, 1905-1973 (E/SB/71); accounts, 1889-1948 (TR); Papers of Leslie Drew, Director of Education, 1937-1975 (D24); programmes for opening ceremonies of schools in Swansea, 1950-1964 (D/D Z 9). See sections below *School Boards and Local Education Authorities* and *School Records* for other records.

Engineer: plans of proposed works submitted under building regulations, *circa* 1925-1965; buildings plans registers, 1860-1951 (BE); planning application registers, *circa* 1948-1962 (PL); registers of applications for building licences, 1945-1954; annual housing returns, 1917-1944; plans of private street works, including sewers, tramways, road improvements and other projects, *circa* 1880-1974 (BE); drawing of the main Swansea drainage system, early 1930s (D33); brochure for the opening of the main drainage works, 1936 (D/D Z 75); transcript of a lecture on the Swansea main drainage scheme (D160); documents concerning drainage and water supply works, 1922-1936 (D54); street lighting plans, 1894 (D61); plans of obsolete street lighting equipment, 1924-1947; Surveyor's report book, 1946-1950; rights of way plan, 1924; photographs, n.d.; general correspondence files, including war damage and post-war reconstruction files (BE)

Estates: title deeds of Corporation property, 1706-1854 (EA 1), 1792-1895 (TC 100); Borough Estate Agent's report books, 1901-1964; accounts, 1918-1948; rentals, 1884-1971 (with gaps); correspondence, 1904-1974; sale catalogues, 1899-1930; photographs, various dates; market accounts, 1941-1968, bye-laws, 1927, and plan, 1956; maps and plans, including Local Board of Health plans of Swansea, 1852-1885, and plan of market buildings, 1895; plans relating to post-war rebuilding, 1945; war damage files, 1940-1969; post-war reconstruction files, 1950-1968 (EA)

Health: annual reports of the Medical Officer of Health, 1889-1965; School Medical Officer reports, 1908-1970; list of returns from the survey of overcrowding of dwelling houses under the Housing Act, 1935 (HE); Port Health Authority: annual reports, 1895-date; financial records, 1885-1958 (PH); Medical Officer of Health reports, 1934-1939 (TC)

Housing: correspondence files (unlisted) (HO); papers concerning the Townhill housing scheme and Harland Engineering *vs* Swansea Corporation, 1922-1926 (TC); artist's impression of Townhill Estate, 1938 (D/D Z 225)

Libraries: account book of Treboeth Public Hall and Library, 1884-1916 (D43). See also section below *Swansea Library Collection* in *Library and Museum Collections*.

Licensing: plan showing distribution of licensed premises, 1939 (D181); documents relating to the licensing of motor vehicles, 1953-1966 (D186)

Parks: meteorological records taken at Victoria Park, 1908-1979 (LE)

Tramways: notes on Swansea's tramways, n.d. (D/D Z 21)

Treasurer: rate books, 1889-1974; abstracts of accounts, annual estimates and budgets, and general accounts, 1889-1974; Assessment Committee minutes, 1927-1950 (unlisted); correspondence, 1894-1900 (TR)

Water: Swansea Local Board of Health Water Works Act, 1860 (D/D Z 299); Swansea Corporation Water Act, 1892 (D/D Z 11); papers relating to a legal case concerning Blaennant Ddu Reservoir, including a history of Swansea Corporation Water Works, 1927 (TC)

URBAN AND RURAL DISTRICT COUNCILS AND LOCAL BOARDS OF HEALTH

In early nineteeth century Britain, sanitary and public health improvements in urban areas, such as there were, were the concern of borough councils, vestries or improvement commissioners (the latter created by private Act). Under the Public Health Act 1848, towns of over 10,000 inhabitants were given powers to set up local boards of health. The Act was adoptive, unless a town had a particularly high death rate, when it could be imposed.

The Public Health Act 1872 made sanitation and public health the concern of urban and rural sanitary authorities. Urban sanitary authorities took over this role from local boards of health, borough councils and improvement commissioners. Rural sanitary authorities were formed from those parts of a poor law union which were outside the control of an urban sanitary authority.

The Local Government Act 1894 enhanced and clarified the powers of sanitary authorities and made them urban and rural districts. Urban and rural district councils existed from 1894 to 1974.

There were originally four urban district councils in West Glamorgan: Briton Ferry, Glyncorrwg, Margam and Oystermouth. Oystermouth Urban District was absorbed into the County Borough of Swansea in 1918, Briton Ferry into the Borough of Neath in 1922. Margam Urban District Council combined with the Borough of Aberavon to form the Borough of Port Talbot in 1921. Of the four rural districts created in 1894, Llangyfelach Rural District Council became in 1902 Swansea Rural District Council. In 1918 parts of Swansea Rural District were lost to the County Borough of Swansea, the remaining parts in 1930 becoming Llwchwr Urban District. The other three rural district councils were Gower, Neath and Pontardawe: all lasted until 1974, although, like all urban and rural districts, they were subject to boundary changes during their period of existence.

See section above *Boroughs* for records of borough councils acting as local boards of health and urban sanitary authorities.

Briton Ferry Local Board of Health

Minutes, 1864-1895 (L/B BF and NL L/B BF); declarations by elected members, 1876-1893 (L/B BF); minutes, 1864-1874; draft minutes, 1864-1895; letter book, 1879-1880; Surveyor's letter book, 1876-1896; register of owners of property and their proxies, 1873-1879; accounts, 1881-1896 (NL L/B BF)

Briton Ferry Urban District Council

Minutes, 1895-1922; committee minutes, 1895-1922 (B/N); correspondence, 1895-1922; Surveyor's records, 1894-1922; Sanitary Inspector's records, 1894-1922; Medical Officer of

UDCs, RDCs and Boroughs, *circa* 1915

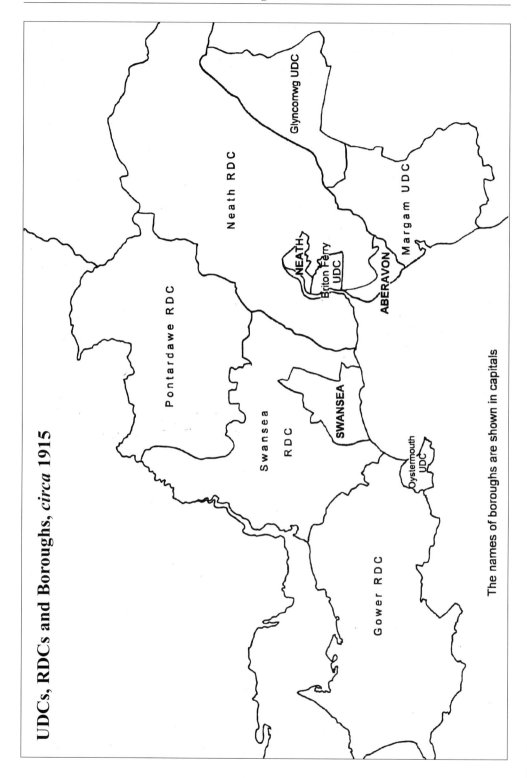

The names of boroughs are shown in capitals

Glyncorrwg UDC

Neath RDC

Margam UDC

NEATH

Briton Ferry UDC

ABERAVON

Pontardawe RDC

Swansea RDC

SWANSEA

Oystermouth UDC

Gower RDC

Health records, 1896-1923; Water Engineer's records, 1897-1922; Treasurer's records, 1886-1961; unlisted material (UD/BF); draft minutes, 1895-1908; letter books, 1898-1922; correspondence, 1890-1921 (unlisted); register of attendance of councillors, 1898-1916; register of motions, 1901; Sanitary Inspector's reports, 1896-1909; Engineer's and Surveyor's letter books, 1892-1896, 1902-1923; accounts, 1880-1885, 1903-1908; Engineer's ledger, 1893-1919; wages records, 1891-1903; planning registers, 1882-1908; registers of explosives, 1891-1920; register of petrol filling stations, 1912-1922; register of omnibus drivers and conductors, 1914-1920; register of cowkeepers and dairymen, 1920-1922; register of dairies, 1906-1922; rate abstracts, 1924-1925; accounts, 1897-1899 (NL UD/BF); staff photograph, 1901 (D/D Z 62)

Glyncorrwg Urban District Council

Minutes, 1893-1974 (1893-1894, Local Board of Health); architectural plans, 1923-1925 (UD/Gl); building regulation plans, 1882-1947 (PTL UD/Gl)

Llwchwr Urban District Council see under *Swansea Rural District Council*

Margam Urban District Council

Minutes, 1897-1921; legal documents, 1898-1939; accounts, 1912-1945; rate books and valuation lists, 1879-1924; building regulation plans, 1919-1920 (UD/Ma); minutes, 1896-1915; deeds and associated records, 1898-1921; accounts, 1912-1918; rating records, 1879-1924; Surveyor's records, 1919-1920 (PTL UD/Ma); Medical Officer of Health reports, 1899-1903 (D/D Xlm)

Oystermouth Local Board of Health

Minutes, 1875-1894; accounts, 1889-1894; miscellaneous papers, 1880-1894 (TC 68)

Oystermouth Urban District Council

Minutes, 1894-1918; accounts, 1894-1905; miscellaneous papers, 1894-1918 (TC 68); rate books, 1897-1915 (UD/Oy); accounts, 1909-1918 (TR); group photograph, n.d. (D88)

Gower Rural Sanitary Authority

Minutes, 1872-1892 (U/G RSA)

Gower Rural District Council

Grant of arms, 1964; minutes, 1910-1972; legal and committee papers, 1931-1974; correspondence, 1945-1974 (TC 69); rate books, 1895-1918 (RD/G), 1941-1955 (TC 69); registers of existing and new dwellings, 1943-1972; accounts, 1950-1974 (TR)

Neath Rural Sanitary Authority

Minutes, 1876-1893 (U/N RSA)

Neath Rural District Council

Minutes, 1894-1973; various committee minutes, 1895-1973 (NL RD/N); legal documents, 1885-1935; accounts, 1919-1971; Medical Officer of Health records, 1919-1973; overcrowding survey, 1936; registers of births reported to the Ministry of Health, 1915-1948; planning and grant application registers, 1881-1974; Parliamentary Acts, 1885-1936 (RD/N); minutes, 1895; cemetery plan, 1915 (PTL RD/N); accounts, 1885-1982 (NM RD/N); applications for tenancy of Glynneath housing site, *circa* 1920 (D/D Z 58)

Pontardawe Rural Sanitary Authority

Minutes, 1883-1893; accounts, 1891-1898 (U/Pd RSA)

Pontardawe Rural District Council

Minutes, 1893-1974; accounts, 1896-1974; rating records, 1922-1958; public health records, 1930-1974; Medical Officer of Health reports, 1927-1933; planning registers, plans and other records, 1925-1973; registers of applications for exemption from military service, 1916; ARP records, 1941-1942; marriage notice books, 1882-1923 (RD/Pd)

Swansea Union Rural Sanitary Authority

Minutes, 1876-1894; accounts, 1874-1894; surveyor's reports, 1884-1896; list of springs, 1889-1901 (U/S RSA)

Swansea Rural District Council, (from 1930, Llwchwr Urban District Council)

Minutes, 1894-1974; accounts, 1898-1974; Public Health Department records, 1934-1983; building and planning registers, 1886-1938 (UD/Lw); papers of Borough Architect T Bryn Richard, relating to the change from rural to urban district, *circa* 1930 (D117)

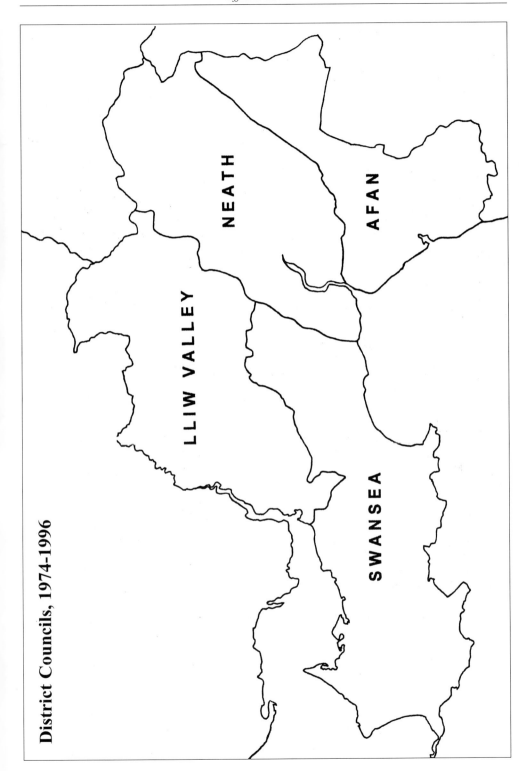

District Councils, 1974-1996

DISTRICT COUNCILS 1974-1996

The Local Government Act 1972 created a two-tier system of local authorities in England and Wales of counties and districts, with counties controlling the major public services and districts those services which were seen as being more suited to provision on a smaller scale. Four districts were created in West Glamorgan: Swansea, from the area of the then City of Swansea combined with Gower Rural District; Lliw Valley, from Llwchwr Urban District and Pontardawe Rural District; Neath, from Neath Borough and Neath Rural District; and Afan, from Port Talbot Borough and Glyncorrwg Urban District.

Under the provisions of the Local Government Act 1972, conurbations were able to petition for borough status and the new district councils of Lliw Valley, Neath and Afan (which later changed its name to Port Talbot) all became boroughs. Swansea retained the title of City, which it had gained in 1969.

District Councils were abolished in 1996, when unitary authorities were created.

Restrictions on access: 30-year rule applies to most record classes.

Borough of Afan see below *Borough of Port Talbot*

Borough of Lliw Valley

Grant of borough status, 1974; grant of arms, 1976; minutes, 1974-1996; reports to committee, 1972-1986; seal registers, 1973-1996; yearbooks, 1974-1996; accounts, 1974-1994; newscutting files, 1974-1995; planning reports, 1978-1992; council house sale case files, 1980-1983 (*closed for 75 years*) (DC/Lli); electoral registers, 1974-1996 (RE/Lli)

Borough of Neath

Minutes, 1974-1986; accounts, 1974-1995; registers of improvement grants, 1974-1987; other records (partly listed) (DC/N); electoral registers, 1974-1996 (RE/N); drawings and report on Gnoll House and Estate, 1985-1987 (B/N);

Borough of Port Talbot (until 1986, Borough of Afan)

Minutes, 1974-1996 (DC/PT); electoral registers, 1974-1996 (RE/PT)

City of Swansea

Grant of borough status, 1973; grant of title of lord mayor, 1982; Lord Mayor's correspondence and engagement files, 1974-1996; visitors' books, 1974-1996; diaries, 1974-1984; minutes, 1974-1996; committee minutes, 1974-1996; bye-laws, various dates; seal registers, 1974-1995; yearbooks, 1974-1996 (TC); electoral registers, 1974-1996 (RE/S); planning reports and accompanying plans, 1974-1996 (PL); posters and leaflets for City of Swansea Leisure Department events, 1985-1996 (SR)

Poster advertising a performance of the Welsh National Opera at the Swansea Grand Theatre, 1982 (TC 323/248)

UNITARY AUTHORITIES

Unitary authorities were created under the Local Government (Wales) Act 1994, which abolished the two-tier system of local government established in 1974. In West Glamorgan, the County Council and the four district councils were all abolished and these five authorities replaced by two new ones, the City and County of Swansea and the County Borough of Neath Port Talbot. The City and County of Swansea comprises the area of the former City of Swansea and the southern part of Lliw Valley Borough. The County Borough of Neath Port Talbot comprises the northern part of Lliw Valley Borough and the Boroughs of Neath and Port Talbot. Few records have as yet been transferred to the Archive Service.

Restrictions on access: 30-year rule applies to most record classes. Most of the records so far transferred are, however, available without restriction.

City and County of Swansea

Grant of arms, 1996; minutes, 1996-date; service delivery plans, 1996-date; staff and community newsletters, 1996-date; Planning Department publications, 1996-date; publicity material relating to the campaign for the Welsh Assembly to be situated in Swansea, 1998 (CC/S); posters and leaflets for City of Swansea Leisure Department events, 1996-date (SR)

County Borough of Neath Port Talbot

(Copy) coat of arms with description, 1996; minutes, 1996-date; service delivery plan, 1996; staff and community newsletters, 1996-date; ephemera, 1996-date (CB/NPT)

CIVIL PARISH AND COMMUNITY COUNCILS

The decline of the manor in the late Middle Ages led to an ecclesiastical division, the parish, becoming increasingly important as a unit of civil administration. From the sixteenth century onwards, unpaid parish officers were responsible for keeping the peace, repairing roads and assisting the poor, by means of a rate levied on the inhabitants of the parish. The controlling body was the vestry.

These responsibilities were lost to other bodies in various nineteenth century reforms, notably to poor law unions and local authorities. The civil parish was reconstituted under the Local Government Act 1894 when parish councils were created with powers over such local matters as recreation grounds and village halls. In 1974, parish councils in Wales became known as community councils.

Typical pre-1894 civil parish records include rate books, accounts and vestry minutes (the latter also relating to ecclesiastical matters). Tithe maps and apportionments date from the years following the Tithe Commutation Act 1836. After 1894, records include minutes, accounts, correspondence and sometimes copies of planning applications.

The Archive Service holds civil parish records for parishes throughout West Glamorgan: brief details and covering dates are given in the alphabetical list below. See the section *Ecclesiastical Parish Records* for other parish records.

Restrictions on access: 30-year rule applies to most record classes.

Aberavon: tithe, 1841 (P/68)

Baglan: accounts, 1784; tithe, 1846; **Baglan Higher Parish (Community) Council (1894-1983):** minutes, 1913-1983; accounts, 1938-1983; correspondence, 1922-1983 (P/69). See also *Pelenna Community Council (1983-)*

Bishopston: tithe, 1844, accounts, 1848-1856 (P/103); **Bishopston Parish Council:** minutes, 1894-1974 (mf)

Blaengwrach: tithe, 1845/6 (P/145)

Cadoxton-juxta-Neath: tithe, 1844; rate book, 1851; lay register, 1638-1679 (P/71)

Cheriton: tithe, 1848; **Cheriton Parish Council:** minutes, 1922-1951 (P/104)

Cilybebyll: tithe, 1840; **Cilybebyll Parish (Community) Council:** minutes, 1894-1989; accounts, 1895-1988 (P/73)

Cockett Parish Council: minutes, 1894-1914; correspondence, 1895-1917 (SL P/325)

Coedffranc: minutes, 1868-1915 (SL P/71)

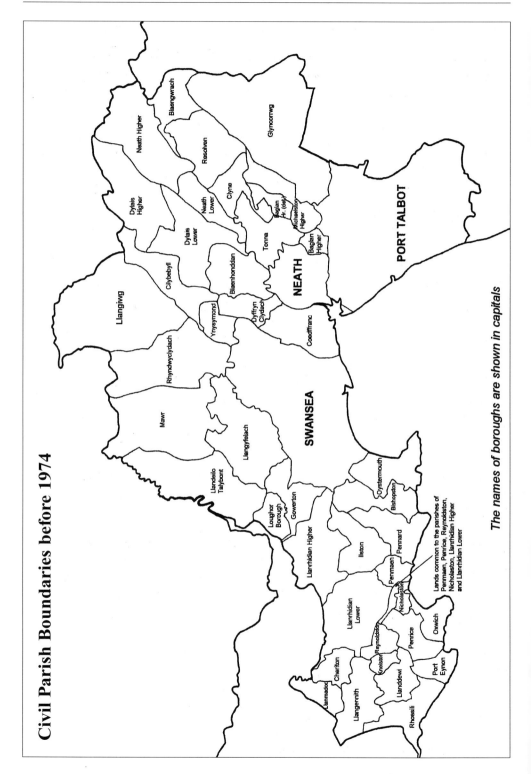

Civil Parish Boundaries before 1974

The names of boroughs are shown in capitals

Dyffryn Clydach Parish (Community) Council: minutes, 1894-1992 (P/242)

Dylais Higher Parish (Community) Council (1894-1983): minutes, 1926-1980; accounts, 1914-1946; correspondence, 1964-1983; papers concerning Brynbedd Cemetery, 1923-1989; papers concerning rights of way and common land, 1958-1974 (P/247). See also *Seven Sisters Community Council (1983-)*

Dylais Lower Parish Council: minutes, 1917-1946; accounts, 1897-1941; correspondence, 1896-1941 (P/246)

Glyncorrwg: tithe, 1847; **Glyncorrwg Community Council:** minutes, 1977-1990; correspondence, 1986-1991; planning applications, 1985-1990 (P/72); history, 1985 (D/D Z 218)

Gowerton Parish (Community) Council: minutes, 1925-1930, 1986-1996 (P/306)

Ilston: tithe, 1844-1846; **Ilston Parish Council:** abstract of rate books, 1927-1945 (P/105)

Killay Community Council: minutes, 1983-1995 (P/307)

Knelston: tithe, 1846 (P/132)

Llanddewi: tithe, 1841 (P/107)

Llandeilo Talybont: tithe, 1844; vestry minutes, 1782-1823, 1884-1894; accounts, 1773-1810; rate book, 1849; Llandeilo Talybont Parish Council: minutes, 1894-1930 (P/108)

Llangennith: tithe, 1847 (P/109)

Llangiwg: tithe, 1842; vestry minutes, 1855-1887; rate books, 1849-1890; electoral list, *circa* 1884; **Llangiwg Parish Council:** minutes, 1894-1897; rate book, 1914 (P/59). See also *Pontardawe Community Council*

Llangyfelach: tithe, 1838; accounts, with vestry minutes, 1809-1894; rate books, 1844-1892; removal orders, 1846; Surveyor's records, 1826-1894; Highway rate books, Mawr Division, 1826-1878; Overseers' accounts, Mawr Division, 1837-1849; **Llangyfelach Parish Council:** minutes, 1894-1930 (P/58). See also *Mawr Parish (Community) Council*

Llanmadoc: tithe, 1845 (P/110)

Llanrhidian: tithe, 1847; vestry minutes, 1833-1894; survey by William Seys, 1652; **Llanrhidian Higher Parish Council:** minutes, 1894-1965; correspondence, 1947-1965; accounts, 1895-1968 (P/111)

Llansamlet: tithe, 1844 (P/160); minutes, 1876-1914; tithe rentals, 1877-1881 (SL P/160)

Llantwit-juxta-Neath: tithe, 1845; accounts, 1800-1865 (P/74)

At A Publick vestry held this 4th day
of august 1825 at velindre Parcel Mawr
place accustomed after been regularly
published in Church concerning a matter
of appeal commenced between John Robert
David Oliver & Jenkin Jones adjour
ned at the last Quarter Sessions at
Neath. It was then and there una
nimously agreed between the Church
warden & Overseer & others the
Parishoners of Parcel mawr of
one part and John Robert & William
Williams, As to chuse and to refer to
two men one on each side to settle
the above matter between them and
in case the referrees should faild on
the above matter another man
is to settle between them the above
matter must be performed in
a fortnight's time from the
above date

Extract from the vestry minute book of Llangyfelach Parish, Parcel Mawr, 1825 (P/58/27)

Loughor: tithe, 1839; vestry minutes, 1863-1889; accounts, 1862-1880; **Loughor Parish Council:** minutes, 1920-1930 (P/112)

Margam: accounts, 1799, 1814-1867; rate books, 1887, 1891 (P/83)

Mawr Parish (Community) Council: minutes, 1894-1978; correspondence, 1895-1915; accounts, 1916-1967; rate book, 1925; plan of Craigcefnparc recreation ground, n.d. (P/58)

Michaelston-super-Avon: tithe, 1839-1841; **Michaelston Higher Parish (Community) Council:** minutes, 1934-1968; accounts, 1942-1983 (P/75)

Neath: tithe, 1845 (P/76)

Nicholaston: tithe, 1844 (P/113)

Oxwich: tithe, 1844; rate book, 1887-1888 (P/114)

Oystermouth: tithe, 1844-1845; rate books, 1870-1908 (P/115)

Pelenna Community Council (1983-): minutes, 1983-1991; accounts, 1983-1992 (P/69)

Penmaen: tithe, 1844-1846 (P/116)

Pennard: tithe, 1846; **Pennard Parish (Community) Council:** minutes, 1953-1993; accounts, 1946-1984 (P/117)

Penrice: tithe, 1846; rate book, 1854-1855; **Penrice Community Council:** minutes, 1983-1987 (P/118)

Pontardawe Community Council: promotional videos, 1995 (P/59)

Port Eynon: tithe, 1846 (P/119)

Reynoldston: tithe, 1838 (P/120)

Rhossili: tithe, 1847; **Rhossili Parish (Community) Council:** minutes, 1943-1976; accounts, 1923-1980 (P/121)

St John-juxta-Swansea: tithe, 1844; rate books, 1852-1905 (P/106)

Seven Sisters Community Council (1983-): accounts, 1983-1984; correspondence, 1983-1987 (P/247)

Swansea St Mary: tithe, 1843; accounts, 1726-1833, including records relating to the parish workhouse 1817-1833; rate books, 1726-1732, 1833-1900 (P/123); list of paupers in Swansea, *circa* 1820 (D/D Xgb)

Tonna Community Council: records (unlisted)

SCHOOL BOARDS
AND LOCAL EDUCATION AUTHORITIES

Education until the late nineteenth century depended on charity and private schools. The demand for universal education was met by the Education Act of 1870 which established school boards to provide elementary education in areas where no such provision existed. School boards were elected bodies, empowered to levy a rate and to establish and maintain schools in districts where voluntary provision was inadequate.

The 1902 Education Act transferred powers for education from school boards to local education authorities (LEAs), which were mostly either county or county borough councils. However, boroughs and urban districts of a certain size had powers over the provision of elementary education under Part III of the Act, and such Part III authorities included Neath and Port Talbot Boroughs. From 1902 to 1944, schools were arranged for administrative purposes into groups, each with its own body of managers.

The 1944 Education Act reformed the 1902 Act, including the way in which education was administered. School Groups were reclassed as Divisions and Part III Education Authorities were abolished, to be replaced by Divisional Executives. In 1974, responsibility for education was transferred completely to county councils.

School board and other administrative records described below consist for the most part of minutes and accounts relating to general education provision, such as staff and premises. Individual school records, including those that relate to pupils, are described in a separate section, *School Records*.

School Boards

Aberavon School Board: minutes, 1893-1903; accounts, 1893-1903 (E/SB/1)

Briton Ferry School Board: minutes, 1888-1905; accounts, 1888-1903 (E/SB/6)

Cilybebyll School Board: minutes, 1871-1903 (E/SB/7)

Clyne School Board: minutes, 1894-1903; accounts, 1899-1903 (E/SB/8)

Cockett School Board: minutes, 1899-1903; accounts, 1901-1903 (E/SB/9); see also *Swansea Higher and Lower School Board* below

Coedffranc School Board: minutes, 1901-1903; accounts, 1893-1903 (E/SB/10)

Dulais Higher School Board: minutes, 1897-1903 (E/SB/16)

Glyncorrwg School Board: minutes, 1890-1903; accounts, 1895-1903 (E/SB/19)

Gowerton School Board: see *Loughor Parish School Board*

Llandeilo Talybont School Board: minutes, 1876-1903; accounts, 1899-1903. **Llandeilo Talybont and Swansea Gorseinon Joint School Board:** minutes, 1895-1903 (E/SB/22)

Llangiwg School Board: minutes, 1875-1903; accounts, 1875-1903 (E/SB/27)

Llanrhidian Higher School Board: minutes, 1873-1903; accounts, 1873-1903 (E/SB/29)

Llansamlet Higher School Board: minutes, 1877-1903 (E/SB/30)

Llantwit Lower School Board: minutes, 1895-1903 (E/SB/33)

Loughor Borough School Board: minutes, 1874-1903; accounts, 1899-1903 (E/SB/35)

Loughor Parish School Board (from 1895, Gowerton): minutes, 1877-1901; accounts, 1895-1903 (E/SB/36)

Margam School Board: minutes, 1881-1903; accounts, 1884-1903 (E/SB/37)

Mawr School Board: minutes, 1892-1903; accounts, 1892-1903 (E/SB/38)

Michaelston Lower School Board: minutes, 1900-1903 (E/SB/39)

Neath School Board: minutes, 1895-1900; accounts, 1880-1920 (E/SB/41)

Neath Higher School Board: minutes, 1884-1903 (E/SB/42)

Oxwich, Penrice and Port Eynon School Board: minutes, 1896-1903 (E/SB/44); accounts, 1882-1906 (D/D P)

Oystermouth School Board: minutes, 1890-1903 (E/SB/45)

Pontardawe School Board: correspondence, 1882-1904 (E/SB/72)

Resolven School Board: minutes, 1897-1903; accounts, 1899-1902 (E/SB/55)

Reynoldston School Board: minutes, 1887-1903; accounts, 1899-1903 (E/SB/56)

Rhossili School Board: minutes, 1875-1903; accounts, 1901-1903 (E/SB/59)

Rhyndwyclydach School Board: minutes, 1875-1903; accounts, 1876-1903 (E/SB/60)

Swansea Higher and Lower School Board: minutes, 1873-1899 (E/SB/63). See also *Cockett School Board* above

Swansea School Board: minutes, 1873-1904 (series continues, see *Borough of Swansea* above); committee minutes, 1889-1904; accounts, 1871-1889 (E/SB/71); correspondence and plan relating to Hafod Schools and Swansea School Board, 1898 (D/D GV)

Ystradgynlais School Board: minutes, 1871-1873 (E/SB/69)

Local Education Authorities 1902-1944

School Groups

Glyncorrwg Group: minutes, 1922-1940 (E/Gl Group)

Gowerton Group: minutes, 1938-1946 (E/Gow Group)

Neath Group: minutes, 1911-1932; accounts, 1919-1922; correspondence, 1918-1944 (E/N Group)

Pontardawe Group: minutes, 1941-1946 (E/Pd Group)

Port Talbot Group: minutes, 1910-1913; correspondence, 1912-1921 (E/PT Group)

Part III Education Authorities

Neath Education Committee: minutes, 1900-1946; correspondence, 1919-1940; accounts, 1903-1915 (E/N Part III)

Port Talbot Education Committee: minutes, 1921-1946; correspondence, 1933-1940; school medical officers' annual reports, 1926-1944; miscellaneous records, 1921-1938 (E/PT Part III)

Local Education Authorities 1944-1974

Neath Division: history of education in Neath Division, 1967 (E/N)

Neath and District Divisional Executive: surveys, 1956 and 1967 (E/N Div)

Local Education Authorities from 1974

West Glamorgan County Council Education Department: school grouping statistics for West Glamorgan schools, 1962-1987 (WGCC/Ed)

See also *Borough of Swansea* in the section *Boroughs* above for records of Swansea Education Committee, 1905-1973

SCHOOL RECORDS

Most of the schools listed below were established after the 1870 Education Act, although the two main charitable providers, known in abbreviated form as National and British schools, are also represented.

Typical records include school log books (a chronological record kept by the head teacher), admission registers and attendance registers. Pupils' names are recorded in the latter two, but are rarely mentioned in the log books. The names of many schools have changed in recent years, particularly replacing English with Welsh placenames. The names used here are the earlier forms, which accord better with the covering dates of the majority of the records, with cross-references from the modern names.

Restrictions on access: school log books and most other records are closed for 30 years; some pupils' records are closed for longer periods.

Elementary Schools

Glyncorrwg Division (E/Gl):

Abercregan: (Infants) log book, 1921-1958

Abergwynfi: (Infants) log books, 1895-1957; (Mixed and Infants, from 1905 Boys) log books, 1882-1948

Cymmer: (Mixed and Infants) log book, 1884-1927; (Boys) log book, 1927-1933; (Senior Mixed) log book, 1933-1945

Glyncorrwg: (Infants) log books, 1885-1977, with loose papers, 1931-1949; (Mixed and Infants) log book, 1869-1885; (Boys) log book, 1885-1916; (Girls) log book, 1885-1897

Tonmawr: admission registers, 1905-1978; HMI reports, 1892-1913

Treshincyn: see *Abergwynfi*

Neath Division (E/N)

Blaendulais: see *Seven Sisters*

Briton Ferry, Brynhyfryd: (Mixed and Infants) log book, 1909-1936

Briton Ferry, Cwrt Sart: (Infants) log book, 1920-1965; (Boys) log book, 1920-1928; (Girls, from 1928 Mixed) log books, 1920-1953

Briton Ferry, Giant's Grave: (Mixed and Infants) log book, 1875-1904

Briton Ferry, Hengwrt: log book, 1958-1983; admission registers, 1958-1993; governors' minutes, *circa* 1981-1988

Briton Ferry, Neath Road: (Infants) log book, 1876-1927; (Boys) log books, 1876-1946; (Girls) log book, 1876-1906; admission and attendance registers, 1902-1968

Briton Ferry, Vernon Place: (Infants) log book, 1894-1947; (Mixed) log book, 1892-1932

Bryncoch: (Mixed and Infants) log books, 1880-1946

Cadoxton: (Infants) log book, 1903-1930; (Mixed) log books, 1863-1883, 1901-1929 (E/N); measured drawing of schools, 1995 (D/D Z 261)

Clyne: (Infants) log book, 1913-1940

Coedffranc: (Infants) log book, 1894-1921; (Girls) log books, 1898-1949; (Senior Mixed) log book, 1950-1952

Crynant (National): (Mixed) log books, 1869-1969; (Infants) log books, 1912-1983; HMI reports, 1871-1881

Cwm Nedd: log book, 1941-1965; admission register, 1870-1910

Glynneath: (Mixed) log books, 1869-1948

Gnoll: (Infants) log book, 1896-1929; (Boys) log books, 1879-1961; (Girls) log books, 1896-1953; **Gnoll Cookery Centre:** log book, 1941-1946; **Gnoll Domestic Subjects Centre:** log book, 1939-1944

Maesmarchog: (Mixed and Infants) log book, 1913-1938; (Junior) log book, 1928-1962

Melin (later Herbert Road): (Infants) log books, 1877-1964; (Boys) log books, 1875-1899; (Mixed) log books, 1899-1938; admission and attendance registers, 1928-1982; miscellaneous records, 1948-1987

Melin (Llantwit Board): (Infants) log book, 1899-1938; (Girls) log books, 1899-1964; admission and other registers, 1917-1967; stock and stores accounts, 1934-1948

Mynachlog Nedd: see *Skewen Lower*

Neath, Alderman Davies (National): (Boys) log books, 1863-1914; (Girls) log books, 1878-1916; (Infants) 1897-1923; admission register, 1912-1933; history, 1958 (E/N); deeds, 1722-1888 (D/D Xge 102)

Neath, St Joseph's (Roman Catholic): (Infants) log book, 1903-1920; (Mixed) log books, 1890-1940

Neath School Society: admission register, 1858-1899

Neath Abbey: (Boys) log book, 1863-1874; (Girls) log book, 1863-1886; (Mixed and Infants) log book, 1886-1922

Neath Upper: (Infants) log book, 1902-1941

Onllwyn: (Mixed and Infants) log books, 1892-1962

Resolven: (Mixed) log books, 1872-1968; (Infants) log books, 1878-1963

Rhigos: (Mixed and Infants) log books, 1876-1926

Seven Sisters (later Blaendulais): (Boys) attendance registers, 1920-1933; (Girls) log book, 1917-1955; admission and attendance registers, 1917-1948; (Mixed) log books, 1884-1958; (Junior Mixed) log book, 1955-1973; admission and attendance registers, 1938-1973; (Infants) log book, 1908-1980; admission and attendance registers, 1923-1972; miscellaneous records, including a history of the schools, 1918-1966

Skewen Lower (National) (later Mynachlog Nedd): (Boys) log books, 1867-1921; (Girls) log books, 1875-1961; (Mixed) log book, 1894-1903

Tonna (National): (Mixed) log book, 1874-1922

Port Talbot Division (E/PT)

Aberavon (National): (Boys) log book, 1901-1922; (Girls) log book, 1895-1922; (Infants) log book, 1874-1922

Aberavon (Unsectarian): (Boys) log books, 1885-1979; (Girls) log books, 1885-1958; (Infants) log book, 1886-1925

Baglan (National): log book, 1865-1949; managers' minutes, 1904-1930

Bryn: (Mixed and Infants) log book, 1886-1913; history, n.d.

Cwmavon: (Boys) log books, 1863-1949; admission register, 1874-1892; (Girls) log books, 1864-1886; admission register, 1876-1881; (Senior Mixed) log book, 1949-1965; (Infants) log books, 1869-1909

Groes: (Mixed and Infants) log books, 1881-1950

Margam Tin Works: (Mixed and Infants) log book, 1874-1899; closed 1899, see also *Port Talbot Central* below

Mountain: see *Aberavon (Unsectarian)*

Park: (Senior Mixed) log book, 1950-1964

Pontrhydyfen: (Mixed and Infants) log books, 1866-1957

Port Talbot Central: (Girls) log book, 1911-1950; (Mixed) log book, 1899-1950; stock and inventory books, 1946-1963

Port Talbot Eastern: (Boys, from 1949 Mixed) log books, 1907-1974; admission registers, 1904-1960 (including entry for Richard Walter Jenkins *alias* Richard Burton); loose papers including letter from Richard Burton's secretary, 1970; (Girls) log books, 1905-1949; admission registers, 1915-1949; (Infants) log books, 1895-1960; admission registers, 1930-1961

Port Talbot Junior Instruction Centre: (Boys) log book, 1930-1940; (Girls) log book, 1937-1939

Sandfields: (Infants) log book, 1885-1940; (Girls) log book, 1915-1951; (Senior Mixed) log book, 1951-1954

Taibach (formerly Margam Copper Works): (Boys) log book, 1893-1907; (Girls) log book, 1868-1902

Tirmorfa: admission registers (Infants), 1956-1981; (Junior), 1957-1995

Traethmelyn: admission registers (Infants), 1963-1980; (Juniors), 1961-1979; census of catchment area, 1960s

Trefelin: (Girls, from 1957 Mixed) log books, 1923-1965; (Infants) log book, 1923-1957

Tymaen: (Infants) log book, 1888-1910 (E/PT); notice of opening, 1855 (D/D Xl)

Swansea Division (E/S)

Aberdyberthi and Bethany: (Mixed and Infants) log book, 1885-1902

Blackpill: (Mixed) log books, 1879-1959; (Infants) log book, 1909-1957

Bryn Mill: (Girls) log book, 1896-1969; admission registers, 1910-1969; (Boys) admission registers, 1936-1947

Brynhyfryd: attendance registers, 1980-1981

Cadle: (Boys) log book, 1953-1956

Cwmbwrla: (Mixed and Infants, from 1879 Boys) log book, 1875-1909; (Girls and Infants, from 1910 Mixed) log book, 1879-1925

Danygraig: (Boys) log books, 1895-1967

Dunvant: log books, 1877-1980; managers' minutes, 1877-1894; admission registers, 1877-1978; miscellaneous records, including photographs, 1915-1994

Dyfatty: (Boys) log books, 1875-1941; admission register, 1927-1941; (Girls) log books, 1893-1941; admission register, 1881-1894; (Girls Cookery) log book, 1912-1919; (Infants) log books, 1892-1933; admission registers, 1924-1979; miscellaneous records, 1969-1979; (Nursery) log book, 1969-1974; admission register, 1969-1979; miscellaneous records, 1968-1978

Gendros: (Senior Girls) log book, 1949-1957; (Mixed and Infants) log books, 1898-1995 (E/S)

Gors: (Infants) log book, 1920-1927

Graig: log books, 1881-1974; admission registers, 1915-1979; photograph album, 1977

Hafod: (Mixed and Infants) log book, 1863-1900

Kilvey: (Boys) log book, 1895-1905

Llansamlet (National): admission registers, 1900-1979

Morriston: (Infants) log books, 1868-1969; admission registers, 1912-1972

Nelson Terrace Nursery: log book, 1955-1969; admission registers, 1944-1954, 1964-1969

Newton: (Mixed and Infants) log books, 1865-1948; admission and attendance registers, 1907-1956; miscellaneous records, 1926-1965

Oxford Street: (Infants) log books, 1887-1932; admission registers, 1873-1882

Pentrechwyth: (Infants) log books, 1863-1929; admission registers, 1915-1963; attendance registers, 1960-1975; staff time book, 1959

Rutland Street: (Boys) log books, 1883-1937

St Helen's: (Junior Partially Sighted Unit): attendance register, 1970-1971

St Thomas: (Girls) log books, 1898-1963; (Infants) log book, 1894-1940

Swansea Parochial: (Boys) log book, 1888-1889; (Girls) log books, 1863-1889; (Mixed) log books, 1863-1928; (Infants) log books, 1863-1928

Tirdeunaw: (Mixed) log books, 1864-1959; (Infants) log book, 1903-1953; (Evening School for Women) log book, 1894-1910

Townhill: (Mixed and Infants) log book, 1923-1937, 1962-1977; admission registers, 1932-1966; miscellaneous records, including photographs, 1927-1977; (Infants) log book, 1927-1979; admission registers, 1927-1974; (Nursery) log book, 1941-1977

Treboeth: (Infants) log book, 1898-1903

Vetch Field: (Girls) log book, 1922-1925; (Infants) log book, 1919-1923

Waun Wen: (Boys) log books, 1873-1938; admission registers, 1929-1950; (Girls) log books, 1899-1948; admission registers, 1932-1948; (Junior Mixed) admission registers, 1948-1964; (Infants) log books, 1875-1970; admission registers, 1902-1972; (Partial Hearing Unit) admission registers, 1964-1966; history of Waun Wen Schools, 1975

York Place: (Girls) log books, 1872-1922; (Infants) log books, 1905-1922

Evacuees: log book of children evacuated from Swansea to Aberduar Vestry School, Llanbydder (Carmarthenshire), 1941; log book of children evacuated from Manselton to Penybont and Trelech (Carmarthenshire), including list, 1941-1942

West Glamorgan Division (E/W)

Plan of West Divisional Area of Glamorgan, showing the location of schools in the area, 1955

Alltwen: (Mixed) log book, 1899-1939; (Infants) log books, 1874-1936

Banwen: (Mixed) log book, 1896-1932; (Infants) log book, 1896-1940

Bishopston: (Mixed and Infants) log books, 1873-1979

Cheriton and Llanmadoc (National): (Mixed and Infants) log book, 1904-1935

Clydach (British): (Senior Mixed) log book, 1937-1951; (Boys) log books, 1884-1937; (Girls) log book, 1887-1934; (Infants) log books, 1875-1966; admission registers, 1880-1975, *circa* 1900-1965

Craigcefnparc (British): (Mixed and Infants) log books, 1869-1913, 1959-1983; admission register, 1962-1993; (Infants) log book, 1909-1950

Crwys: see *Three Crosses*

Cwmllynfell (British): (Mixed) log books, 1863-1931; (Infants) log books, 1863-1953

Felindre: see *Velindre*

Garnswllt: log books, 1873-1986; census register, *circa* 1931-1951; correspondence, 1925-1939

Godre'rgraig: (Mixed) log book, 1882-1908

Gorseinon: (Boys) log books, 1893-1938; (Girls) log books, 1907-1967; (Infants) log book, 1893-1926

Gowerton: (Boys) log books, 1896-1952; (Girls) log books, 1894-1952; (Mixed) log book, 1880-1895; (Infants) log book, 1880-1903

Grovesend (later Pengelli): (Infants) log book, 1916-1938; (Senior Mixed) log book, 1917-1962

Gwaun-Cae-Gurwen: (Mixed and Infants) log book, 1867-1878; (Infants) log books, 1879-1936; (Mixed) log book, 1879-1930; (Senior Mixed) log books, 1935-1958

Gwrhyd: (Mixed and Infants) log book, 1890-1906

Kingsbridge (later Pontybrenin): (Infants) log book, 1908-1952

Knelston: see *Reynoldston*

Llandeilo Talybont (National): (Mixed and Infants) log books, 1882-1923; (Infants) log book, 1923

Llangyfelach: (Mixed and Infants) log books, 1880-1921

Llanmorlais: (Mixed and Infants) log book, 1893-1935

Llanrhidian Lower: (Mixed and Infants) log books, 1879-1979

Loughor Lower: (Mixed and Infants) log books, 1882-1967

Loughor Upper (National) (later Treuchaf): (Girls) log book, 1917-1952; (Mixed and Infants) log book, 1863-1900; (Mixed) log books, 1901-1952; (Infants) log books, 1866-1928

Oystermouth: (Mixed) log books, 1878-1960; admission registers, 1878-1937

Oxwich: (Mixed and Infants) log books, 1884-1961; admission register, 1882-1961; accounts, 1948-1960; correspondence, 1956-1961; miscellaneous records, *circa* 1895-1932

Pantteg: log books, 1877-1910; admission register, 1948-1974; (Infants) log book, 1877-1929

Parkmill: (Mixed and Infants) log books, 1872-1956

Penclawdd: (Mixed) log book, 1863-1909; (Infants) log books, 1875-1945

Penclyn: (Mixed and Infants) log books, 1880-1930; admission registers, 1880-1930

Pengelli: see *Grovesend*

Penllergaer: (Mixed and Infants) log books, 1881-1970; admission registers, 1906-1965; stock and inventory book, 1939-1955

Penmaen (National): (Mixed and Infants) log books, 1875-1944

Penyrheol: (Mixed and Infants) log books, 1880-1930; (Infants) log book, 1909-1945

Pontardawe: (Mixed, then Boys) log books, 1863-1951; punishment book, 1921-1939; accounts, 1903-1939; correspondence, 1926-1939; (Girls) log books, 1900-1964; punishment book, 1900-1943; attendance summaries, 1898-1904; stock and inventory book, 1920-1946; (Infants) log book, 1863-1895

Pontarddulais: (Senior Mixed) log book, 1938-1947; (Senior Mixed and Infants) log book, 1878-1894; (Junior Mixed) log book, 1894-1903; (Boys) log book, 1922-1938; (Infants) log books, 1878-1936

Pontlliw: (Mixed and Infants) log book, 1913-1947

Pontybrenin: see *Kingsbridge*

Port Eynon (National): (Mixed and Infants) log book, 1906-1946

Reynoldston (later Knelston): (Mixed and Infants) log book, 1874-1907; (Junior) log book, 1907-1969

Rhossili: (Mixed and Infants) log book, 1882-1911

Rhiwfawr: (Mixed and Infants) log books, 1906-1979

Rhydyfro: (Mixed and Infants) log book, 1877-1931; admission register, 1877-1911; history, 1977

Tairgwaith: (Infants) log books, 1900-1938

Three Crosses (later Crwys): (Mixed and Infants) log books, 1875-1927; (Infants) log books, 1911-1963

Trebanos (later Trebannws): (Mixed) log books, 1884-1984; admission registers, 1938-1983; (Infants) log books, 1884-1964; admission registers, 1908-1955; (Old Council School) log book, 1916-1921

Treuchaf: see *Loughor Upper*

Velindre (later Felindre): (Mixed and Infants) log books, 1877-1991; attendance registers, 1932-1944; punishment books, 1915-1927; accounts, 1934-1957

Waunarlwydd: log books, 1864-1981; (Infants) log books, 1883-1967

Wern: (Boys) log books, 1863-1960; (Girls) log book, 1893-1933; (Infants) log books, 1863-1939

Out-county

Ystradgynlais (National): building accounts, including list of subscribers, 1813-1816 (D/D Yc)

Secondary Schools

County secondary schools were established under the Welsh Intermediate Education Act of 1889 and were transferred to local education authorities in 1902. Most secondary schools have gone through several name changes. The names used here are, wherever appropriate, those used prior to the introduction of comprehensive education.

Bishop Gore School (formerly Swansea Grammar School): deeds, 1682-1683 (D18); minutes, 1888-1894; registers of scholars, 1851-1894; history, 1853; magazines, 1897; photographs, *circa* 1870-1952 (E/BG Sec); bond, 1848 (D/D Z 154); article on the opening of the school, 1853 (D/D Xgb)

Clydach Boys' Council School: admission register, 1937 (E/Cly Sec)

De-la-Beche Girls' Secondary School, Swansea: log book, 1930-1942 (E/D G Sec)

Dunvant Secondary School: log book, 1948-1969; admission registers, 1947-1969 (E/S)

Dynevor Secondary School, Swansea: magazines, 1957-1970; miscellaneous records, 1920-1984 (E/Ll B Sec)

Glanmor Girls' Grammar School, Swansea: log book, 1922-1972; magazines, 1947-1962; programmes for school concerts etc, 1930-1965 (E/S and E/Gla Sec)

Gowerton County School: Governors' minutes, 1896-1945; accounts, 1923-1939 (E/Gow Sec)

Gowerton Grammar Schools: (Boys) log book, 1937-1968; admission registers and indexes, 1901-1963; staff registers, 1897-1946; inspection reports, 1926-1937; examination results, 1924-1968; circulars and miscellaneous records, 1926-1957; photographs (unsorted) (E/Gow Sec); school magazines, 1961-1985 (D/D X 192); (Girls) visitor's book, 1948-1957; magazines, 1948-1972 (E/Gow G Sec)

Ysgol Gyfun Gwyr, Gowerton: history, 1995 (E/Gyf/Gw)

Gwaun-Cae-Gurwen County Secondary School: log books, 1958-1990 (E/W)

Llwyn-y-Bryn Girls' High School, Swansea: log book, 1950-1976; staff registers, 1895-1976; admission register, 1895-1925; pupil registers, 1924-1972; summary attendance register, 1945-1963; pupil's report books, 1934-1972; pupil's record cards, 1918-1977 (*closed for 60 years*); examination results, 1937-1974; photographs, *circa* 1890-1956; magazines, 1933-1973 (E/Ll B Sec)

Manselton County Secondary School, Swansea: (Girls) log books, 1902-1965; admission registers, 1902-1965; (Boys) admission registers, 1902-1970 (E/S)

Morriston Girls' County Secondary School: log books, 1892-1970; admission registers, 1899-1970 (E/S)

Neath Girls' County Grammar School: accounts, 1938-1973; history, 1946 (E/N G Sec)

Neath Intermediate School: minutes, 1912-1951; admission registers, 1905-1972; staff register, 1896-1939 (E/Nea Sec)

Neath Technical Secondary School: minutes, 1951-1960 (E/Nea Tech Sec)

Oxford Street Secondary Schools, Swansea: (Boys) log books, 1886-1940, 1947-1977; admission registers, 1947-1961, 1970-1977; punishment books, 1957-1976; (Girls) log books, 1863-1940; admission register, 1898-1906; history of the schools, 1948 (E/S)

Pen-y-bryn School, Swansea see *Cambrian Institution*

Penclawdd Secondary Modern School: log books, 1971-1973 (E/Pen Sec)

Pontardawe Secondary School (formerly Higher Elementary): log book, 1913-1965 (E/W); minutes, 1913-1929 (E/Pd Sec);

Port Talbot County School (later, Glanafan): history, 1996 (E/PT Sec)

Port Talbot Intermediate School: minutes, 1924-1949; accounts, 1919-1948 (E/PT Sec)

St Helen's Girls' County Secondary School, Swansea: log books, 1874-1969; admission registers, 1940-1969 (E/S)

St Thomas' Girls' Secondary School, Swansea: history, 1963 (E/STG Sec)

Swansea Girls' Secondary Technical School, Cockett: log book, 1955-1969; admission register, 1955-1969 (E/S Sec Tech)

Swansea Grammar School: see *Bishop Gore School*

Swansea Secondary Technical School: history, 1997 (E/S Sec Tech)

Townhill Boys' Secondary School, Swansea: log books, 1927-1979 (E/S)

Ynysfach Secondary School: attendance registers, 1950s (E/N)

Ystalyfera County Grammar School: minutes, 1896-1955; correspondence, 1896-1913; admission registers, 1896-1955; accounts, 1892-1946; headmaster's records, 1892-1969 (*closed for 60 years*); photographs, 1943-1962 (E/Yst Sec)

Ysgol Gyfun Ystalyfera: history, 1994 (E/Gyf Yst)

Colleges of Further Education

Cwmavon Mechanics' Institute: list of members and officers, 1849-1851 (D/D Xk)

Neath Technical College: minutes, 1932-1973; correspondence file, 1955-1973; photograph, 1949 (E/Nea/Tech)

Swansea Training College: staff register, 1892-1976; teacher's certificate (E/Coll/S)

Neath Borough and District Evening Classes: minutes, 1927-1945 (E/N/Ev)

Special Schools

Glamorganshire Reformatory School (later Glamorgan Farm School): minutes, 1907-1947; log book, 1958-1966; admission and discharge registers, 1892-1984 (with gaps); other records, 1891-1983 (partly listed) (GCC/E/GFS, *restricted access:* only by prior written permission from the County Archivist)

Cambrian Institution for the Deaf and Dumb (later Pen-y-bryn School, Swansea): minutes, 1847-1887; reports, 1860-1876; accounts, 1849-1860; correspondence, 1876-1909; photograph, 1955 (E/Cam)

University College Swansea

Annual reports, 1920-1994; calendars, 1955-1991; handbooks, 1964-1985; prospectuses, 1929-1980; College gazette, 1965-1967 (D/D UCS); photograph, *circa* 1925-1935 (D/D Z 12)

Other records relating to individual schools

Building Grant Plans

Architectural plans of primary schools, *circa* 1840-1892, submitted to central government for educational building grants, including the following: Aberavon National; Briton Ferry National; Bryncoch National; Cadoxton National; Cheriton, Llanmadoc and Llangennith National; Clydach National; Crynant National; Llandeilo Talybont National; Loughor National; Morriston British; Neath Alderman Davies Charity; Neath School Society British; Neath Abbey British; Neath Abbey National; Neath Higher National; Neath Higher National; Penclawdd National; Pontardawe; Swansea National; Swansea Goat Street British; Swansea Queen Street British Girls; Swansea St David's Roman Catholic; Swansea St Peter's National (D/D PRO/EBG)

County Council Education Department Plans

Plans of Glamorgan schools, 1892-1939, including the following: Abercregan; Abergwynfi; Alltwen; Banwen; Blaengwrach; Blaengwynfi; Bryncoch; Cadoxton; Cilybebyll; Clydach; Clyne; Cockett; Craig Trebanos; Crynant; Cwmavon; Cwmgors; Cymmer; Cymmer Afan; Dunvant; Glyncorrwg; Glynneath; Gors; Gorseinon; Gowerton; Grovesend; Gwaun-Cae-Gurwen; Jersey Marine; Killay; Kingsbridge; Llandeilo Talybont; Llanrhidian; Loughor; Maesmarchog; Neath; Neath Mining Institute; Neath Ty-Segur Farm School; Onllwyn; Oystermouth; Pantteg; Parkmill; Penclawdd; Penclyn; Penllergaer; Pontardawe; Pontardawe Mining Institute; Pontarddulais; Pontlliw; Port Talbot; Resolven; Reynoldston; Rhos; Seven Sisters; Skewen; Taibach; Tairgwaith; Three Crosses; Tonmawr; Tonna; Trebanos; Trefelin; Wern; Ystalyfera (C/C E Pl)

Glamorgan County Council School Compendia

Details of accommodation and various provisions in individual schools, 1932, including a plan of the school, for the following: Abercregan; Aberdulais; Abergwynfi; Alltwen; Banwen; Bishopston; Blaengwrach; Bryncoch; Cadoxton; Cilfrew; Clydach; Clyne; Coedffranc; Craigcefnparc; Crynant; Cwmgors; Cwmllynfell; Cymmer Afan; Duffryn Afan; Garnswllt; Glyncorrwg; Glynneath; Godre'rgraig; Gorseinon; Gowerton; Gwaun-Cae-Gurwen; Jersey Marine; Killay; Kingsbridge; Llangyfelach; Llanmorlais; Llanrhidian; Lower Loughor; Maesmarchog; Neath Abbey; Onllwyn; Oxwich; Pantteg; Penclawdd; Pengelli; Penllergaer; Penmaen; Pennard; Penyrheol; Pontardawe; Pontarddulais; Pontlliw; Port Eynon; Resolven; Reynoldston; Rhigos; Rhiwfawr; Rhos; Rhossili; Rhydyfro; Seven Sisters; Skewen; Tairgwaith; Three Crosses; Tonmawr; Tonna; Trebanos; Upper Loughor; Velindre; Wern; Ynysmeudwy (GCC/E Comp)

Brochures for opening ceremonies

Programmes for opening ceremonies of schools in Swansea, 1950-1964 (D/D Z 9 and D/D Z 254)

Joseph Lancaster Exhibitions

A Charity Commission scheme to administer the proceeds for the sale of the Queen Street British School, Swansea, was issued in 1889 under the name of the Joseph Lancaster Exhibitions. The charity assisted girls wishing to train as teachers.

Minutes, 1889-1935; accounts 1889-1938; correspondence, 1889-1946; Board of Education scheme for alteration of regulations, 1915 (E/Ex/W)

Entrance fee?

Register of Scholars.

Name of Scholar, *Henry Morris Greening*

Names of Parents, *Charles Greening & Catherine Eaton*

Profession, *Wheelwright*

Residence, *Upper Killay, Gower, near Swansea*

Date of Entering, *January 12, 1881*   Date of Leaving,

Admitted on *payment as a Day Scholar*

Age on Entering, *18 years* ——— Age on Leaving,

Previous Master and School, *Chas. Revd. Cryer, Sketty Natl. Schools.*

Attainments on Entering, *Not learnt Latin or Greek or French: has entered for the purpose of being prepared for the Univy of Cambridge!!*

conduct very good.

Progress and Conduct in the School, *very slow, progress scarcely preceptible Easter 1881 // "beginning to break the ice", he thinks, but I doubt his capacity to acquire learning equals his ambition. Is very dull July 1881 // Progress slow Xmas 1881 // progress slow, because "thawing" a little; conduct excellent Easter 1882 // not much advancement perceptible July 1882 // Dull & heavy Xmas 1882 // works away like a Trojan, trying to get a fig out of a thistle Easter 1883 // industrious July 1883 // absent half the term from ill health Xmas 1883 // absent all the term, Easter '84 // went to Cambridge Oct 1884, having been with us last term //*

General Remarks. *I wish he would pay his school bill. He will not be allowed to continue at Cambridge on the same principle.*
He has kept all his terms at Downing Coll, Cambridge, but never passed any exams. (1870)

John Young   HEAD MASTER.

Register No. *55*

Entry from the register of scholars of Swansea Grammar School, 1881 (E/BG Sec 1/2)

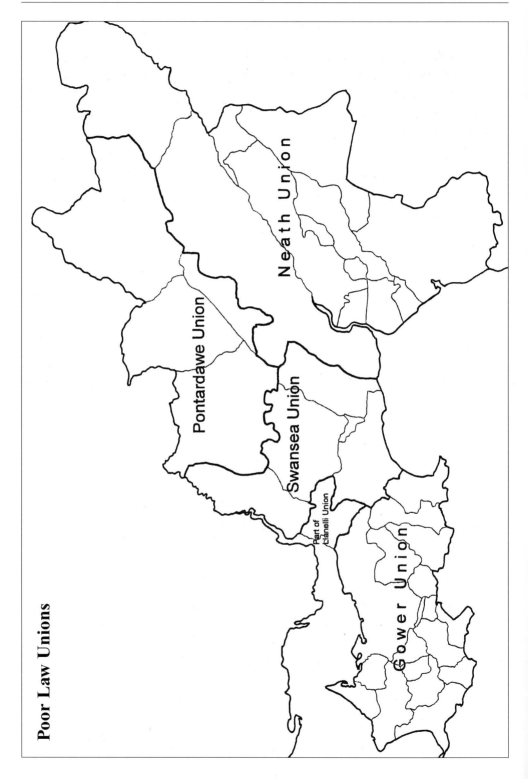

Poor Law Unions

Neath Union

Pontardawe Union

Swansea Union

Part of Llanelli Union

Gower Union

POOR LAW UNIONS

The Elizabethan Poor Law placed responsibility for the care of the poor on individual parishes. Following the Poor Law Amendment Act of 1834, parishes were combined into larger units, known as poor law unions. Administered by boards of guardians, each union was empowered to build its own workhouse. Four unions were created in West Glamorgan: Gower, Swansea, Pontardawe and Neath.

The poor law union proved to be a conveniently-sized unit of local administration: additional duties were allotted to them after 1834 unrelated to poor relief, including civil registration, vaccination and rate assessment. In 1872, unions in rural areas took on powers for public health as rural sanitary authorities (later to become rural district councils). Poor law unions were abolished in 1930, when their powers were taken over by county councils and county boroughs.

Poor law union records include the typical minutes, accounts and correspondence of an administrative body. There are also rate books and, occasionally, vaccination registers. Workhouse records contain details of inmates, their diet and the regulations by which they were governed. Records of rural sanitary authorities are described above in *Urban and Rural District Councils and Local Boards of Health.*

The Parish of Loughor formed part of the Llanelli Union, and records relating to this union will be found at the Carmarthenshire Record Office

Restrictions on access: Records relating to individuals are closed for 100 years

Gower Union

Minutes, 1896-1930; accounts, 1895-1930; Gower Union Workhouse: title deeds, 1860-1866; registers, 1869-1949; day books, 1922-1949; accounts, 1915-1952 (U/G); accounts, 1916-1924 (TR); plan and conveyance for workhouse at Penmaen, 1858-1860 (D/D Xau)

Neath Union

List of paupers in Parish of Margam, 1842 (D/D Xlm); minutes, 1853-1930; accounts, 1917-1930; vaccination registers, 1853-1947; Neath Union Workhouse: registers, 1867-1940; report books, 1917-1930; accounts, 1912-1946; Bryncoch Cottage Homes: registers, 1877-1955; accounts, 1901-1949 (U/N)

Pontardawe Union

Minutes, 1875-1930; accounts, 1875-1930; valuation lists, 1897-1927; Pontardawe Union Workhouse: registers, 1902-1943; day books, 1933-1949; accounts, 1875-1949 (U/Pd).

Glamorgan County Council Public Assistance Committee: minutes, 1931-1936; registers, 1933-1962; accounts, 1929-1958 (GCC/PAC/Pd)

Swansea Union

Minutes, 1849-1930; correspondence, 1859-1869; valuation lists, 1863-1928 (U/S); rate books, 1845-1918; accounts, 1866-1949 (TR); photograph of Board of Guardians, 1895 (D178); Swansea Union Workhouse: master's reports, 1842-1914; registers, 1836-1954; accounts, 1838-1927; Cockett Cottage Homes: Visiting Committee books, 1878-1904; report books, 1883-1950; accounts, 1878-1905 (U/S)

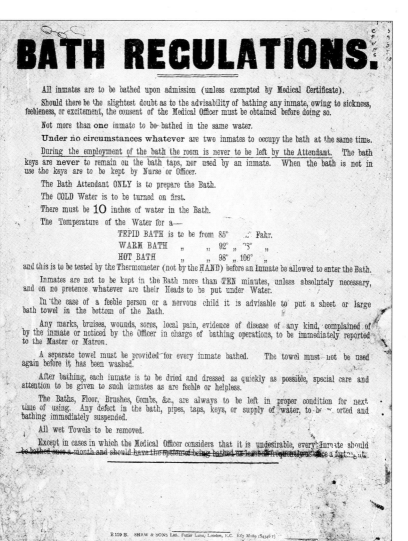

Printed regulations concerning the taking of baths, Pontardawe Union Workhouse, circa 1920 (U/Pd 28)

HIGHWAY AND BURIAL BOARDS

The development of boards to deal with public works and matters of public health was part of the *ad hoc* development of local government in the nineteenth century. Highway boards were established in rural areas under powers granted by the General Highway Act 1835 and the Highways Act of 1862, transferring responsibility for the upkeep of roads to themselves from parish vestries. Highway boards were taken over by rural sanitary authorities after 1878.

In order to deal with overcrowded parish and chapel graveyards, under the Burial Acts of 1852 and 1853, burial boards were established which were able to administer their own cemeteries. Such boards were abolished under the Local Government Act 1894 and their duties transferred to the new district and parish councils. Some of the records listed below are of later date because the new authorities continued to use the same series of books.

Municipal cemetery records are retained by the Burials and Cremations Sections in each of the two present local authorities.

Highway Boards

Neath District Highway Board: minutes, 1855-1895 (H/B N)

Pontardawe Highway Board: minutes, 1889-1894; accounts, 1876-1889 (H/B Pd)

Swansea Highway Board: minutes, 1886-1892; accounts, 1890-1892 (H/B S)

Burial Boards

Briton Ferry Burial Board: minutes, 1879-1922 (Bu/B BF); register of burials and graves, 1880-1896; accounts, 1896-1907 (NL Bu/B BF)

Neath Burial Board: correspondence (unlisted) (NL Bu/B N)

Swansea Burial Board: ledger, 1890-1912; plan of burial grounds in Swansea, 1891 (Bu/B S); minutes, 1854-1911; correspondence, 1854-1862; register of burials, Danygraig Cemetery, 1865-1870 (TC 70)

RULES

OF THE

SWANSEA ASSOCIATION,

For the Profecution of Felons, &c.

ASSENTED TO BY

Mr. R. AWBREY,	Mr. J. PHILLIPS,
Mr. W. DAVIES,	Mr. T. MORGAN,
Mr. D. WILLIAMS,	Mr. B. ROSE,
Mr. T. ALLEN,	Mr. D. PERROTT,
Mr. S. LLEWELYN,	Mr. J. A. SIMONS, and
Mr. W. SPENCER,	Mr. J. VOSS, *Treafurer*,

Who have formed themfelves into a COMMITTEE *to tranfaćt the Bufinefs of the* SOCIETY *for the enfuing Year.*

THAT each Member fhall pay down the Sum of *Two Shillings and Six-pence* on entering his Name, and the like Sum annually at *Lady-day* or *Michaelmas*; and if any Member fhall fail to pay his Subfcription within Fifteen Days after every *Lady-day* or *Michaelmas*, fuch Perfon fhall receive no Benefit from this SOCIETY.

THAT this SOCIETY fhall pay the Expences of advertizing, taking, and profecuting, any Perfon or Perfons who fhall rob, felonioufly defraud, or otherwife injure the Perfon or Property of any or either of the Subfcribers.

THAT when any of the SOCIETY fhall be robbed, or otherwife injured in his Perfon or Property, he is immediately to apply in Perfon or by Letter to the *Treafurer*, who fhall with the Concurrence of any Four of the Committee, take fuch Steps to purfue, advertize, apprehend and profecute, fuch Offender or Offenders, as to them fhall appear expedient.

WHERE there are Two or more Partners, they are entitled to the Benefit of this SOCIETY, when Goods their joint Property, are ftolen or obtained from them by Fraud, if *Two Shillings and Six-pence* only be fubfcribed; but not in Cafes of Robbery on the Highway, or other Robberies of their feperate private Property, unlefs each Partner fubfcribe *Two Shillings and Six-pence.*

THAT no Attorney's Bill, or Fees to Council fhall be allowed, unlefs they are employed under the Direćtion of the Committee.

THAT the *Treafurer* be empowered to call the Committee together on any Matter of Importance: And that any Five of them be deemed a Committee, and their Decifion fhall be final and conclufive.

THAT no Member who may be robbed or defrauded, fhall be entitled to have his Expences paid out of the common Stock, unlefs he makes his Claim to the fame within Three Months after the Termination of the Profecution.

SWANSEA, 13th *February,* 1792.

[TYP. T. GOODERE.]

Rules of the Swansea Association for the Prosecution of Felons, 1792 (D/D Xgb 13/1)

POLICE RECORDS

Records of the Glamorgan County Constabulary, 1841-1969, are held at the Glamorgan Record Office, Cardiff. The County Borough of Swansea had its own police force until 1969. In 1969, several forces combined to form the South Wales Constabulary.

Swansea Association for the Prosecution of Felons

Rules, 1792; accounts and list of subscribers, 1818 (D/D Xgb)

Swansea Constabulary

History, 1957 (D/D Con/S); volume of photographs of criminals at Swansea Police Station, 1893-1905 (D74) (*restricted access:* only by prior written permission from the County Archivist); bye-laws, orders and general instructions, 1915 (D146); Local Acts and bye-laws, 1938 (D/D Z 20); aliens' registration records, *circa* 1930-1972 (unlisted: *closed until 2020*)

South Wales Police Authority

Minutes and reports, 1973-date; photograph, 1995 (D/D SWPA)

SOUTH WALES SEA FISHERIES COMMITTEE

The local sea fisheries committees of England and Wales were set up under the Sea Fisheries Regulation Act 1888, to regulate the sea fisheries inside territorial waters. Each local committee consisted of persons appointed by its constituent local authorities together with an equal number of members appointed to represent the fishing interests.

The South Wales Sea Fisheries District Committee was created in 1912. Before that, there were two sea fisheries committees in South Wales, the Glamorgan Sea Fisheries District Committee, set up in 1890, and the Milford Haven Sea Fisheries Committee, set up in 1892. The order combining the two district committees into a single committee made the new committee responsible for an area which extended from Cardiff to Cardigan. The local authorities represented on the South Wales Sea Fisheries District Committee were the County Councils of Carmarthenshire, Glamorgan and Pembrokeshire and the County Boroughs of Cardiff and Swansea.

Local committees were empowered to make bye-laws restricting the activities of the fishing industry, controlling the shellfish industry, and regulating discharges into the sea. They were also authorised to enforce various acts and orders which had relevance to the welfare of fish and of the fishing industry.

Of particular interest among the papers of the South Wales Sea Fisheries Committee are various reports relating to the cockle industry of the Loughor estuary, to oyster culture, to the effect on the South Wales fishing industry of the military firing ranges in the locality, and to the problems posed by oil pollution and the discharge of sewage and industrial waste into the sea along the South Wales coastline (D/D SWSF).

Glamorgan Sea Fisheries District Committee: correspondence with the Board of Trade and the Board of Agriculture and Fisheries, 1893-1912

Milford Haven Sea Fisheries District Committee: accounts, 1906-1913

South Wales Sea Fisheries District Committee: constitution and functions of the South Wales Sea Fisheries Committee, including lists of members and chairmen, 1949-1965; minutes, 1912-1978; sub-committee minutes, 1913-1976; reports of Clerk and Chief Fishery Officer, 1946-1976; MAFF statistics, 1924-1980; Acts of Parliament, Fishery Orders and bye-laws, 1868-1973; register of licences under the Swansea Fishery Order, 1892-1935; day books of fishery officers, 1949-1959; accounts, 1940-1980; correspondence files, 1903-1983

ECCLESIASTICAL PARISH
RECORDS

The Ancient Parishes

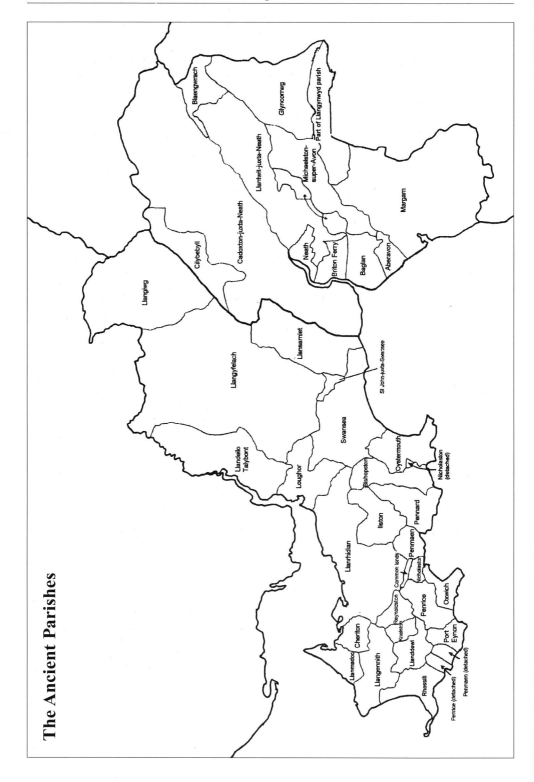

ECCLESIASTICAL PARISH RECORDS

The West Glamorgan Archive Service was appointed, under the 1976 Agreement between the Representative Body of the Church in Wales and the Welsh County Councils, as the recognised repository for parishes in the Archdeaconry of Gower in the Swansea and Brecon Diocese. The majority of these parishes have now deposited their older records with the Service, although a small number (mostly Gower parishes) have deposited their records in the National Library of Wales. The Archive Service has purchased microfilm copies of registers for the latter parishes. The few parishes which have not yet deposited records are nineteenth and twentieth century creations and have records less than 100 years old. Records of West Glamorgan parishes in the Diocese of Llandaff are held by the Glamorgan Record Office, Cardiff: the Archive Service holds facsimile copies of most of these registers

Baptism, marriage, banns and burial registers are the most used of all parish records and are essential sources for the study of family history. Although orders about the keeping of registers date from 1538 and 1597, in practice the earliest extant West Glamorgan registers are all of seventeenth century date. Remoteness from central government and the vicissitudes of time have combined to ensure that earlier registers were either not kept or have been lost.

Parish registers held at the Record Office have all been photocopied and are available in facsimile form in the archive searchroom. Covering dates for the registers are given below (the first set of dates after the parish name). Where the Archive Service does not hold an original register from a West Glamorgan parish, a facsimile copy or microfilm is usually available. These are marked (F) and (mf) respectively. Facsimile copies are also held of registers of many parishes in the rest of the historic county of Glamorgan, as are parish register indexes and memorial inscriptions where these have been compiled by the Glamorgan Family History Society. Bishop's Transcripts for ancient West Glamorgan parishes are available on microfilm: the originals of these are in the National Library of Wales, together with other diocesan records. The covering dates for microfilm of Bishop's Transcripts are given in the list below, marked with the abbreviation (BT).

Other ecclesiastical parish records include, typically, service registers, churchwardens' accounts, vestry minutes and parochial church council records. Some parishes have records of local charities and church schools. The covering dates for records other than registers are given below, marked (R).

See above *Civil Parish and Community Councils* for information on civil parish records, including tithe, highways and poor relief.

Restrictions on access: None for registers. 30-year rule applies to parish records other than registers

Aberavon: 1747-1955 (F); 1696, 1722-1837 (BT)

Abercrâf: 1912-1989; 1874-1945 (R)

Aberdare St John: 1734-1946 (F)

Aberdare St Elvan: 1855-1937 (F)

Abergwynfi: 1914-1985 (F)

Aberpergwm: 1837-1987 (F)

Afan Vale: 1907-1916 (F)

Baglan: 1769-1904 (F); 1721, 1723-1837 (BT)

Barry: 1724-1958 (F)

Bettws: 1722-1963 (F)

Bishopston: 1716-1965 (mf); 1671-1838 (BT)

Blaengwrach: 1837-1988 (F)

Bonvilston: 1758-1983 (F)

Briton Ferry: 1668-1969 (F); 1696, 1721-1837 (BT)

Briton Ferry St Thomas: 1936-1965 (F)

Cadoxton-juxta-Barry: 1752-1951 (F)

Cadoxton-juxta-Neath: 1638-1965 (F); 1721-1837 (BT)

Callwen: 1685-1977; 1935-1973 (R)

Canton St John: 1858-1868 (F)

Cardiff St Andrew: 1863-1954 (F)

Cardiff St Dyfrig: 1885-1894 (F)

Cardiff St John: 1735-1921 (F)

Cardiff St Mary: 1843-1907 (F)

Cardiff St Stephen: 1912-1925 (F)

Cardiff St Teilo: 1884-1921 (F)

Cheriton: 1672-1841 (transcript only); 1671-1837 (BT)

Cilybebyll: 1638-1931 (F); 1721-1837 (BT)

Clydach St John: 1847-1987

Clydach St Mary: 1905-1988; 1903-1987 (R)

Clydach St Michael, Trebanos: 1912-1970

Coelbren: 1863-1990; 1925-1985 (R)

Cogan: 1786-1979 (F)

Colwinston: 1949-1983 (F)

Cowbridge: 1718-1972 (F)

Coychurch: 1736-1959 (F)

Crynant: 1838-1942 (F)

Cymmer: 1927-1981 (F)

Dowlais: 1839-1855 (F)

Dunvant: 1897-1957

Dyffryn: 1871-1970 (F)

Eglwys Brewis: 1750-1970 (F)
Eglwysilan St Cenydd, Senghenydd: 1909-1947 (F)
Eglwysilan St Peter, Senghenydd: 1898-1917 (F)
Flemingston: 1726-1968 (F)
Gelligaer: 1813-1933 (F)
Gelligaer St Margaret, Gilfach: 1907-1923 (F)
Glantawe St Margaret, Bonymaen: 1931-1983; 1938-1987 (R)
Glantawe St Peter, Pentrechwyth: 1967-1979; 1910-1991 (R)
Gileston: 1701-1812 (F)
Glyncorrwg: 1813-1988 (F)
Glyntaff: 1848-1887 (F)
Gorseinon Holy Trinity: 1883-1978; 1881-1977 (R)
Gorseinon St Catherine: 1913-1986; 1908-1984 (R)
Gowerton: 1882-1970; 1893-1959 (R)
Gwaun-Cae-Gurwen: 1892-1976 (F)
Ilston: 1653-1812 (mf); 1672-1838 (BT)
Killay: 1923-1980
Kilvey: 1845-1971; 1849-1944 (R)
Knelston: 1784-1794 (BT)
Laleston: 1742-1971 (F)
Landore: 1891-1933; 1890-1930 (R)
Lisvane: 1755-1980 (F)
Llanblethian: 1734-1971 (F)
Llandaff: 1874-1968 (F)
Llanddewi: 1718-1978; 1678-1837 (BT); 1754-1974 (R)
Llanddewi Rhondda: 1897-1916 (F)
Llandeilo Talybont: 1662-1960 (mf); 1672-1837 (BT)
Llandough-juxta-Cowbridge: 1583-1986 (F)
Llandow: 1839-1969 (F)
Llanedeyrn: 1701-1978 (F)
Llanedeyrn All Saints, Cyncoed: 1926-1979 (F)
Llangan: 1792-1984 (F)
Llangennith: 1726-1993 (mf); 1671-1836 (BT); 1844-1924 (R)
Llangiwg: 1703-1979; 1672-1837 (BT); 1799-1967 (R)
Llangiwg All Saints, Pontardawe: 1887-1979
Llangiwg St Mary, Ynysmeudwy: 1913-1988
Llangiwg St Peter, Pontardawe: 1862-1985; 1887-1954 (R)
Llangyfelach: 1693-1975; 1795-1837 (BT); 1749-1971 (R)
Llangynwyd: 1662-1769 (F)
Llanharan: 1837-1984 (F)

Llanharry: 1813-1983 (F)

Llanilid: 1706-1987 (F)

Llanishen: 1813-1914 (F)

Llanmadoc: 1724-1837 (mf); 1672-1835 (BT)

Llanmaes: 1583-1812 (F)

Llanrhidian: 1730-1930 (mf); 1671-1838 (BT)

Llanrumney St Dyfrig: 1970-1979 (F)

Llansamlet: 1704-1992; 1672-1837 (BT); 1780-1972 (R)

Llansamlet St John, Birchgrove: 1931-1986

Llansamlet St Paul, Glais: 1884-1977

Llansawel: 1913-1965 (F)

Llantrisant: 1837-1962 (F)

Llantwit Fardre: 1754-1972 (F)

Llantwit-juxta-Neath: 1638-1919 (F); 1698-1837 (BT)

Llwynderw: 1908-1988; 1899-1991 (R)

Llwynderw Church of the Holy Cross, West Cross: 1961-1986; 1956-1988 (R)

Llysworney: 1754-1970 (F)

Loughor St David: 1950-1982

Loughor St Michael: 1717-1994; 1669-1837 (BT); 1835-1989 (R)

Loughor St Paul, Garden Village: 1950-1971

Manselton: 1906-1978; 1897-1988 (R)

Marcross: 1813-1986 (F)

Margam: 1672-1953 (F)

Margam Chapel of Ease, Port Talbot: 1850-1895 (F)

Matthewstown and Ynysboeth: 1903-1971 (F)

Merthyr Mawr: 1749-1981 (F)

Merthyr Tydfil: 1813-1835 (F)

Michaelston-super-Avon: 1785-1930 (F); 1696, 1723-1837 (BT)

Monknash: 1754-1987 (F)

Morriston St David: 1891-1990; 1864-1981 (R)

Neath: 1638-1900 (F); 1721, 1723-1837 (BT)

Neath St David: 1867-1902 (F)

Newcastle: 1745-1943 (F)

Newton: 1903-1993; 1899-1993 (R)

Nicholaston: 1787-1985; 1671-1837 (BT); 1814-1971 (R)

Oxwich: 1772-1984; 1672-1837 (BT); 1824-1947 (R)

Oystermouth: 1719-1954 (mf); 1672-1837 (BT)

Penclawdd: 1835-1992; 1854-1959 (R)

Penllergaer: 1851-1987; 1911-1988 (R)

Penmaen: 1765-1985; 1681-1837 (BT); 1820-1974 (R)

Penmark: 1751, 1755-1985 (F)
Pennard: 1743-1971 (mf); 1677-1837 (BT)
Penrhiwceiber: 1829-1986 (F)
Penrice: 1631-1970; 1677-1837 (BT); 1846-1928 (R)
Pentyrch: 1837-1946 (F)
Peterston-super-Ely: 1749-1966 (F)
Pontyclun with Talygarn: 1903-1953 (F)
Port Eynon: 1740-1970; 1672-1837 (BT); 1837-1982 (R)
Porthkerry: 1754-1970 (F)
Pyle and Kenfig: 1695-1925 (F)
Radyr: 1916-1963 (F)
Resolven: 1850-1969 (F)
Reynoldston: 1713-1993; 1682-1837 (BT); 1843-1963 (R)
Rhossili: 1641-1978; 1671-1837 (BT); 1884-1926 (R)
Roath: 1837-1904 (F)
Roath St German: 1884-1927 (F)
Rudry: 1755-1935 (F)
St Athan: 1677-1964 (F)
St Bride's Major: 1723-1831 (F)
St Bride's Minor: 1813-1949 (F)
St Bride's-super-Ely: 1747-1970 (F)
St George's-super-Ely: 1693-1984 (F)
St Hilary: 1690-1985 (F)
St John-juxta-Swansea: 1797-1974; 1785-1837 (BT); 1823-1990 (R)
St Lythan's: 1749-1985 (F)
St Mary Church: 1584-1985 (F)
St Mary Hill: 1738-1985 (F)
St Nicholas: 1762-1930 (F)
Sketty: 1850-1984; 1850-1995 (R)
Skewen: 1850-1993 (F)
Sully: 1754-1812 (F)
Swansea Christ Church: 1872-1971; 1872-1938 (R)
Swansea Holy Trinity: 1856-1941; 1842-1958 (R)
Swansea St Barnabas: 1915-1971; 1929-1997 (R)
Swansea St Gabriel: 1889-1994; 1886-1989 (R)
Swansea St Gabriel (St Augustine's Chapel of Ease): 1905-1994
Swansea St James: 1867-1985; 1860-1994 (R)
Swansea St Jude: 1896-1988; 1887-1986 (R)
Swansea St Luke, Cwmbwrla: 1886-1989; 1890-1980 (R)
Swansea St Mark: 1888-1978; 1887-1984 (R)

Swansea St Mary: 1631-1989; 1676-1837 (BT); 1739-1991 (R)

Swansea St Matthew: 1886-1992

Swansea St Matthew (Greenhill Mission): 1918-1962; 1905-1924 (R)

Swansea St Nicholas: 1886-1920; 1865-1921 (R)

Swansea St Nicholas-on-the-Hill: 1924-1989; 1937-1980 (R)

Swansea St Nicholas-on-the-Hill (Good Shepherd Mission): 1927-1946

Swansea St Peter, Cockett: 1856-1943; 1855-1923 (R)

Swansea St Phillip: 1886-1976 (R)

Swansea St Thomas: 1888-1990; 1886-1993 (R)

Swansea St Thomas, Port Tennant Chapel of Ease: 1903-1959

Tongwynlais: 1879-1971 (F)

Tongwynlais St James, Taff's Well: 1897-1971 (F)

Treboeth: 1928-1989; 1909-1980 (R)

Treharris St Cynon: 1863-1971 (F)

Treharris St Matthias: 1900-1945 (F)

Tycoch: 1966-1991; 1957-1986 (R)

Tythegston: 1758-1987 (F)

Waunarlwydd: 1888-1992; 1906-1988 (R)

Welsh St Donat's: 1726-1982 (F)

Wenvoe: 1740-1983 (F)

Whitchurch: 1732-1944 (F)

Wick: 1754-1812 (F)

Ystalyfera St David: 1890-1991; 1913-1970 (R)

Ystalyfera Holy Trinity, Godre'rgraig: 1859-1979; 1913-1938 (R)

Ystradfellte: 1754-1970; 1920-1970 (R)

Ystradgynlais: 1721-1990; 1854-1989 (R)

Ystradyfodwg St David, Ton Pentre: 1920-1986 (F)

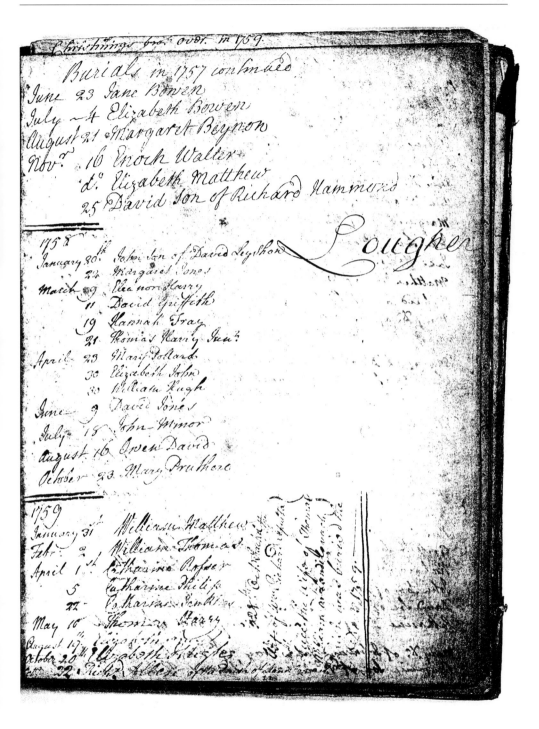

Extract from the burial register of Loughor Parish, 1757-1759 (P/112/CW/2)

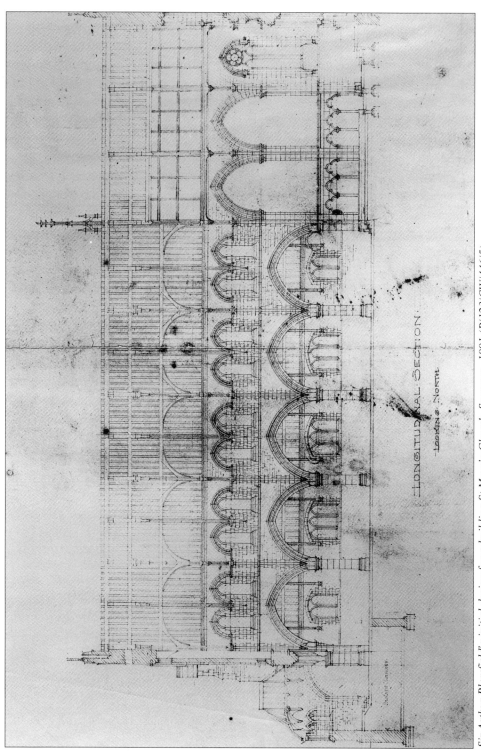

Sir Arthur Blomfield's initial design for rebuilding St Mary's Church, Swansea, 1891 (P/123/CW/446/5)

NONCONFORMIST
RECORDS

NONCONFORMIST RECORDS

The nonconformist denominations came into being from the seventeenth century onwards as a result of differing theological interpretations of scripture and consequently of worship and church government. The main seventeenth century sects in England were the Baptists, Presbyterians and Independents, together with the much smaller Society of Friends or Quakers. Most of these sects played a part in the religious history of Wales, although the principal ones were the Baptists and Independents. The eighteenth century saw the rise of Methodism, which broke from the Established Church and in turn split into several divisions, the two most important being Wesleyan and Calvinistic Methodism. In Wales, the Calvinistic Methodists later became the Presbyterian Church of Wales.

The first Baptist church in Wales was established at Ilston on the Gower peninsula in 1649. Baptist churches are generally self-governing within a Baptist Union. There are separate Baptist Unions for English and Welsh speaking congregations.

Welsh Independent chapels have for the most part remained separate from the English-based Congregational Union and the United Reformed Church (created in 1972 from a union of English Congregational and Presbyterian churches). They belong to a loose association, the Union of Welsh Independents (Annibynwyr).

The history of nonconformity in Wales is one of steady growth in the eighteenth century and explosive expansion in the nineteenth, with communities having at least one chapel, often several vying for prominence in inter-denominational rivalry. Baptist and Independent congregations are self-governing, whereas the Wesleyan Methodist and Welsh Presbyterian Churches have a central administration. This affects both the form and the survival of their records. Apart from registers, typical records include contributions books and other accounts, deeds and trust papers, minutes and Sunday School records. Many chapel histories have been written, particularly in celebration of the centenary of a chapel building. A chapel photographic survey detailed below, undertaken during the early 1990s, includes internal and external views of surviving chapels in West Glamorgan, including chapel buildings now used for other purposes.

A number of nonconformist registers were surrendered to the Registrar General under the Non-Parochial Registers Act of 1840, and a second series in 1857. These volumes are now in the Public Record Office and the Archive Service holds photocopies of the originals. Such items are marked in the list below as 'PRO copy'.

Restrictions on access: None for registers. 30-year rule applies to records other than registers.

BAPTIST

Carmel Baptist Chapel, Aberdare: births, 1806-1837 (PRO copy)

Aberdulais Baptist Chapel: marriages, 1983-1992

Jerusalem English Baptist Chapel, Briton Ferry: register of members, 1863-1893; dismission books, 1898-1982; correspondence, 1949-1970; deeds, 1866-1952; accounts, 1870-1972; newscuttings, 1933-1974; photographs, *circa* 1880-1983; plans, 1906-1970; Sunday School records, 1923-1966; records of the Independent Order of Rechabites, *circa* 1913 (D/D Bap); history, 1959 (D/D Z 81)

Bethany Baptist Church, Cardiff: births, 1804-1837 (PRO copy)

Capel y Tabernacl, Cwmrhydyceirw: centenary programme, 1994

Bethel Baptist Chapel, Glyncorrwg: marriages, 1971-1988

Ilston Baptist Church: register of members and minutes, 1650-1844 (photocopy: original in USA)

Siloam Baptist Church, Killay: church history, 1981

Bethel Baptist Chapel, Georgetown, Merthyr Tydfil: births, 1810-1837 (PRO copy)

Seion Newydd Welsh Baptist Chapel, Morriston: chapel histories, 1946 and 1995

Soar Baptist Chapel, Morriston: ephemera, 1908-1958 (D/D Z 313)

Bethany Baptist Chapel, Neath: births, 1773-1837 (PRO copy)

Calfaria Baptist Church, Port Talbot: annual reports, 1910-1952; contribution books, 1914-1958; accounts, 1928-1953; orders of service, 1933-1958; Sunday School registers, 1931-1954; correspondence of the Caradog ap Iestyn Lodge of True Ivorites, 1913-1916

Bethesda Baptist Chapel, Swansea: marriage registers, 1900-1977

Swansea General Baptist Church: deeds, 1758-1852

Memorial Baptist Church, Swansea: marriages, 1953-1991; photographs, 1992

Mount Pleasant Baptist Chapel, Swansea: births, 1813-1837 (PRO copy)

Townhill Baptist Church, Swansea: baptisms and dedications, 1928-1967, 1982; communion register, 1929-1950; minutes, 1928-1979; accounts, 1932-1984; correspondence, 1939-1986; deeds, 1933-1986; architect's plans, 1932-1949; Sunday School records, 1960-1969; photographs, 1933-1952

York Place English Baptist Church, Swansea: births, 1830-1837 (PRO copy); minutes, 1830-1947; members' roll, 1855-1947; magazines, 1901-1905

Bethany English Baptist Church, Waunarlwydd: minutes, 1878-1937; church history, 1975

Moriah Chapel, Ynystawe: minutes, 1931-1991; contributions register, 1926-1994

Caersalem Chapel, Ystalyfera: marriage registers, 1954-1988

Soar Chapel, Ystalyfera: chapel history, 1943

(D/D Bap unless otherwise specified)

INDEPENDENT
(WELSH CONGREGATIONAL)

Tabernacle Chapel, Aberavon: baptisms, 1822-1837 (PRO copy)

Y Wern, Aberavon: history, 1943 (D/D Z 295)

Salem Chapel, Aberdare: baptisms and burials, 1790-1837 (PRO copy)

Danygraig Chapel, Alltwen: marriage registers, 1949-1995

Alltwen Congregational Chapel: baptisms, 1760-1837 (PRO copy)

Tabernacle and Bethel Chapels, Bridgend: baptisms, 1785-1789, 1818-1837 (PRO copy)

Bethesda Chapel, Briton Ferry: registers of contributions, 1859-1981; accounts, 1910-1970; Sunday School records, 1906-1908

Ebenezer Chapel, Cardiff: baptisms, 1818-1837 (PRO copy)

Hebron Chapel, Clydach: baptisms, 1808-1837 (PRO copy)

Tabernacle and Bethel Chapels, Coychurch: baptisms, 1810-1837 (PRO copy)

Cwmaman Chapel: baptisms, 1760-1835 (PRO copy)

Zion Chapel, Cwmavon: marriage registers, 1908-1988

Seion Chapel, Cwmllynfell: baptisms, 1751, 1760-1835; list of persons admitted to communion, 1767-1772; petitions, 1760-1769 (PRO copy)

Ebeneser Chapel, Cwmtwrch: chapel history, 1992

Hebron Chapel, Cymmer: register of members, 1797-1859

Bethany Chapel, Dowlais: baptisms, 1825-1837 (PRO copy)

Bryn Sion and Bethel Chapels, Dowlais: baptisms, 1829-1837 (PRO copy)

Ebeneser Chapel, Dunvant: chapel history, 1972

Nebo Church, Felindre: agreement for rebuilding, 1857; members' subscriptions, 1867-1881 (D/D Z 27)

Craig Bargoed Chapel, Gelligaer: baptisms, 1832-1837 (PRO copy)

Saron Chapel, Gendros: minutes, 1905-1989; accounts, 1903-1937; deeds, 1917; annual reports, 1906-1989; correspondence, 1910-1989; list of deacons, 1905-1955; chapel histories, 1935 and 1955

Siloh Chapel, Landore: baptisms, marriages and burials, 1918-1940; Sunday School history, 1922

Y Maendy Chapel, Llanblethian: baptisms, 1803-1837 (PRO copy)

Mynydd-bach Chapel, Llangyfelach: baptisms, 1794-1837 (PRO copy); deeds, 1761-1975 (D17); marriage register, 1983-1984; register of graves, 1876-1994; transcript of register, 1676-1784

Bethlehem Chapel, Llanharan: baptisms, 1777-1814, 1830-1837 (PRO copy)

Bethel Chapel, Llansamlet: baptisms, 1794-1837 (PRO copy); marriages, 1983-1987; photograph, *circa* 1910

Bethesda Chapel, Llantwit Major: baptisms, 1798-1837 (PRO copy)

Horeb Chapel, Loughor: marriage registers, 1942-1980; history, 1958 (D/D X 35)

Carmel Chapel, Maesteg: baptisms, 1807-1837 (PRO copy)

Siloh Chapel, Melincryddan: deeds, 1879-1946; history, 1982

Adullam Chapel, Merthyr Tydfil: baptisms, 1833-1837 (PRO copy)

Bethesda Chapel, Merthyr Tydfil: baptisms, 1809-1837 (PRO copy)

Zoar Chapel, Merthyr Tydfil: baptisms, 1810-1837 (PRO copy)

Libanus Chapel, Morriston: baptisms, 1809-1837 (PRO copy)

Gnoll Road Congregational Church, Neath: deacons' minutes, 1893-1904

Maesyrhaf Chapel, Neath (to 1965): registers of members and contributions, 1824-1965; minutes, 1918-1965; accounts, 1844-1965; Sunday School records, 1915-1953; photograph, *circa* 1900 (D/D Ind); history, 1923 (D/D Z 81). **Zoar Chapel, Neath (to 1965):** register of contributions, 1932-1964; minutes, 1927-1964; accounts, 1953-1969; chapel reports, 1916-1965; chapel history, 1963. **Zoar-Maesyrhaf Chapel, Neath (from 1965):** registers of contributions, 1965-1977; minutes, 1965-1977; annual reports, 1966-1975; chapel history, 1995; Sunday School records, 1959-1977

Capel yr Onllwyn: marriage register, 1981-1991; graveyard survey, 1992; register of contributions, 1913 and 1927; accounts, 1904-1927; Sunday School records, *circa* 1919-1924; photographs, 20th century; chapel history, 1994

Paraclete Chapel, Oystermouth: baptisms, 1820-1836 (PRO copy)

Siloam Chapel, Pentre Estyll: baptisms, burials and list of members, 1936-1959; minutes, 1908-1967; annual reports, 1901-1968; accounts, 1893-1976; Sunday School records, 1875-1980; histories, 1933 and n.d.

Hermon Chapel, Plasmarl: marriage register, 1973-1991

Soar Chapel, Seven Sisters: marriages, 1904-1995; burials, 1890-1995; register of graves, n.d.; deed, 1923; annual reports, 1901-1994; correspondence, 1972-1990; chapel histories, 1951 and 1972; cymanfa ganu programmes, 1902-1995; photograph, 1993

Bethel Chapel, Sketty: chapel history, 1993

Castle Street, Swansea: baptisms, 1836-1837 (PRO copy)

Ebenezer Congregational Church, Swansea: chapel history, 1954

Walter Road Congregational Church, Swansea: baptisms, 1930-1981; members' roll, 1867-1949; minutes, 1867-1971; accounts, 1871-1883; annual reports, 1882-1942 (D211); history, 1969 (D/D Z 295)

Noddfa Chapel, Taibach: Band of Hope pledge book, 1945

Capel y Crwys, Three Crosses: chapel history, 1988

Bryn Seion Chapel, Tonmawr: chapel history, 1947

Pantteg Chapel, Ystalyfera: baptisms, 1822-1837 (PRO copy); annual reports, 1949-1989; chapel histories, 1921 and 1971 (D/D X 125)

(D/D Ind and D/D W Cong unless otherwise specified)

ENGLISH CONGREGATIONAL AND
UNITED REFORMED CHURCH

Gendros English Congregational Church, Fforestfach: chapel history, 1995

Hill United Reformed Church, Swansea: history, 1981

Manselton United Reformed Chapel: history, 1997 (D/D Z 295)

Peniel Green English Congregational Church, Llansamlet: church history, 1985

Bethel United Reformed Church, Sketty: history, 1993 (D/D Ind)

St Andrew's United Reformed Church, Swansea: baptisms, 1864-1884, 1898-1991; marriages, 1957-1992; burials, 1864-1881; communicants' roll books, 1963-1973; minutes, 1862-1992; accounts, 1889-1967; trustees' papers, 1876-1985; annual reports, 1935-1972; photographs 1864-1962; magazines, 1927-1976 (D212)

St Paul's Congregational Church, Swansea: pew rent book, 1888-1912

Walter Road Congregational Church, Swansea: baptisms, 1930-1981; members' roll, 1867-1949; minutes, 1867-1971; accounts, 1871-1883; annual reports, 1882-1902, 1912-1942 (D211); history, 1969 (D/D Z 295)

(D/D E Cong unless otherwise specified)

WELSH WESLEYAN METHODIST

The Archive Service is the official repository for the records of the present-day Morgannwg Circuit, which encompasses an area from Cardiff to Carmarthen.

South Wales District records: Chapel Loan Fund account books, 1873-1970; schedules of Methodist Trust property, 1947-1964

Circuit records (now all belonging to Morgannwg Circuit):

Abercynon Circuit: register of deeds, 1929

Cardiff Circuit: schedule of property, 1949-1966

Carmarthen Circuit: accounts, 1849-1883; schedule of property, 1861-1881; circuit diagram, 1883-1884

Llandeilo Circuit: baptism registers, 1863-1975; schedule of property, 1950-1966

Llanelli Circuit: baptism register, 1888-1915; burial register, 1849-1910; minutes, 1916-1937; schedule of property, 1888-1923

Merthyr Tydfil Circuit: baptism registers, 1807-1837 (PRO copy), 1906-1968

Morgannwg Circuit: schedule of property, 1960-1981

Swansea Circuit: baptism registers, 1810-1930; minutes, 1879-1966; schedule of property, 1944-1959; accounts, 1809-1960

Swansea and Llanelli Circuit: circuit plans, 1966-1968

Tredegar Circuit: deeds, 1906-1940; correspondence, 1956-1963

Chapel records:

Capel Carmel, Abercynon: accounts, 1893-1989

Capel Wesley, Tirydail, Ammanford: minutes, 1913-1960; accounts, 1946-1973

Capel Zoar, Bedlinog: miscellaneous papers, 1889-1936

Capel Ebenezer, Brynmawr (Monmouthshire): trust documents, 1860-1977

Capel Bethel, Caerau: trust papers, 1906-1974

Capel Bethel, Cardiff: minute book, 1937-1971; correspondence, 1963-1977

Capel Ebenezer, Carmarthen: legal correspondence, 1860-1974

Capel Bethel, Clydach: stock records, 1889-1943

Capel Bethel, Crynant: trust papers, 1920-1967; chapel history, 1983

Capel Bethcar, Ebbw Vale: correspondence, 1907-1957

Capel Rehoboth, Gorseinon: appointment of new trustees, 1947; plan, n.d.

Gurnos Chapel: accounts, 1839-1854

Capel Soar, Hirwaun: trust papers, 1886-1966

Capel Bethesda, Kidwelly: accounts, 1911-1935

St Paul's Chapel, Llandeilo: property records, 1910-1988

Llandybie Chapel: trust papers, 1884-1975

Jerusalem Chapel, Llanelli: trust papers, 1921-1937; chapel history, *circa* 1940

Capel Zion, Mynydd Bach (Carmarthenshire): trust papers, 1905-1971

Capel Bethel, Nantyglo: trust papers, 1909-1982

Capel Ebenezer, Neath Abbey: accounts, 1885-1989; minutes, 1897-1980; trust papers, 1833-1963

Capel Hermon, Pembrey: trust papers, 1884-1994; baptisms, 1822-1915

Capel Horeb, Pontardawe: minutes, 1920-1963; contribution books, 1883-1926; correspondence, 1888-1976; rules for burial, 1916 and 1925

Capel Triniti, Pontarddulais: accounts, 1890-1973; minutes, 1932-1942; Sunday School records, 1887-1972; photographs, *circa* 1890-1910

Capel Salem, Pontlottyn: correspondence, 1897-1966

Tabernacle, Rhymney: trust papers, 1854-1953

Capel Bethesda, Sirhowy (Monmouthshire): accounts and correspondence, 1871-1910

Bible Christian Chapel, Skewen: deed, 1909

Capel Tabernacle, Swansea: trustees' minutes, 1909

Hendy Chapel, Tafarnaubach (Monmouthshire): trust papers, 1939-1953

Llwynyronnen, Trapp (Carmarthenshire): contribution books, 1960-1973; trust papers, 1808-1974

Capel Ebenezer, Tredegar: insurance documents, 1846-1939; trust papers, 1854-1947

Tumble Chapel (Carmarthenshire): accounts, 1920-1948
Capel Seion, Ystalyfera: correspondence, 1933-1985
Capel Rhiwbina, Cardiff: trust papers, 1954-1970

(D/D W/Wes)

ENGLISH WESLEYAN METHODIST

Circuit records

Neath Circuit: minutes, 1897-1968; quarterly meeting minutes, 1895-1986; trustees' minutes, 1866-1960; preachers' minutes, 1862-1902; record book, 1963-1981; circuit schedules, 1866-1965; accounts, 1862-1917; membership roll, 1931-1941; Sunday School records, 1869-1909; Home and Foreign Mission accounts, 1930-1953
Swansea and Gower Circuit: baptism register, 1864-1913

Church records

Bethel, Aberavon: marriage registers, 1932-1962
Zion, Aberavon: marriage registers, 1907-1963
Abercregan: marriage registers, 1937
Aberdulais: trustees' minutes, 1901-1911; leaders' meeting minutes, 1938-1976; collection journal, 1913-1925; accounts, 1910-1978
Abergwynfi: collection journal, 1914-1923
Briton Ferry: trustees' minutes, 1891-1953; accounts, 1925-1957; collection journal, 1920-1925, 1968-1983
Crynant: accounts, 1858-1911
Cwmavon: marriage registers, 1938-1971; accounts, 1847-1872
Cwmgors: marriage register, 1959-1968
Glynneath: minutes, 1930-1983; accounts, 1930-1984
Gorseinon: baptism register, 1955-1964
Landore: marriage registers, 1948-1988; chapel history, 1961
Morriston: marriage registers, 1940-1949
Murton: baptism register, 1893-1976
London Road, Neath: marriage registers, 1909-1971; members' register, 1912-1924; minutes, 1898-1983; collection journals, 1894-1921; accounts, 1847-1980; Sunday School records, 1925-1977
Windsor Square, Neath: minutes, 1909-1971; accounts, 1889-1974; correspondence, 1912-1924; Sunday School records, n.d.

Ebenezer, Neath Abbey: marriage registers, 1918-1981

Pitton: chapel history, 1987

Pontardawe: marriage registers, 1924-1977

Sketty: chapel history, 1976

Skewen: marriage register, 1907-1934; trustees' minutes, 1877-1882, 1936-1985; leaders' meeting minutes, 1950-1980; accounts, 1904-1938

Alexandra Road, Swansea: marriage registers, 1904-1933

Brunswick Chapel, Swansea: baptism registers, 1867-1991; chapel histories, 1923 and 1973

Goat Street, Swansea: chapel history, 1990

Oxford Street, Swansea: marriage registers, 1920-1940

Pell Street, Swansea: marriage registers, 1908-1940; deeds, 1859-1860

St Alban's Road, Swansea: baptisms, 1904-1976; marriages, 1919-1969

Townhill, Swansea: marriage registers, 1955-1978

Swansea Wesley Mission: baptism register, 1941-1952

Taibach: leaders' meeting minutes, 1893-1905

(D/D Wes/A, D/D Wes/N and D/D Wes/SG)

PRESBYTERIAN CHURCH OF WALES
(CALVINISTIC METHODIST)

Carmel Chapel, Aberavon: baptisms, 1815-1837 (PRO copy)

Tabernacle Chapel, Aberthaw: baptisms, 1818-1837 (PRO copy)

Nazareth Chapel, Birchgrove: baptisms, 1900-1992; burials, 1900-1992; contribution book, 1897-1919

Capel y Cwm, Cadoxton-juxta-Neath: baptisms, 1820-1837 (PRO copy)

Bethel Chapel, Clase: baptisms, 1811-1837 (PRO copy)

Hermon Chapel, Dowlais: baptisms, 1828-1837 (PRO copy)

Capel y Cwm, Llansamlet: baptisms, 1812-1837 (PRO copy)

Ebeneser Chapel, Llansamlet: marriages, 1972-1989

Tabernacle, Llantwit Major: baptisms, 1812-1837 (PRO copy)

Pontmorlais Chapel, Merthyr Tydfil: baptisms, 1807-1837 (PRO copy)

Bethlehem Green Chapel, Neath: baptisms, 1811-1837 (PRO copy)

Clawdd Coch Chapel, Pendoylan: baptisms, 1821-1837 (PRO copy)

Sardis Chapel, Penmark: baptisms, 1818-1837 (PRO copy)

Y Capel, Skewen: marriages, 1983-1994

Hermon Chapel, Skewen: marriages, 1971-1988

Argyle and Rhyddings Park Chapels, Swansea: chapel histories, 1993

Gorse Mission Forward Movement Hall, Swansea: marriages, 1982-1984

Jerusalem Church, Ravenhill, Swansea: minutes, 1910-1960 (D/D Z 66)
Trinity Chapel, Swansea: baptisms, 1808-1837 (PRO copy)
Dyffryn Chapel, Taibach: baptisms, 1815-1837 (PRO copy)
Dyffryn Ajalon Chapel, Taibach: marriages, 1972-1989
St Nicholas, Trehill: baptisms, 1823-1836 (PRO copy)

(D/D CM unless otherwise specified)

FREE CHURCH

Swansea Free Church Council: minutes, 1889-1982 (D/D FC)
Swansea Gospel Mission: attendance registers, 1876-1900; journals and notebooks, 1864-1887; correspondence, 1872-1876 (SL GM)

APOSTOLIC CHURCH

Records (partly listed); history of the Apostolic movement, including sections on the development of the movement in South Wales, 1991 (D/D Ap)

UNITARIAN

Records of the Swansea Unitarian Congregation, 1930-1985, including a register of baptisms, marriages and deaths, 1930-1969 (D/D Un)

Papers relating to Unitarians in South Wales, 19th century (SL DRP)

SOCIETY OF FRIENDS

Society of Friends' records for South Wales Monthly Meeting are held at the Glamorgan Record Office, Cardiff. The original of the microfilm below is held at Friends House Library, London.

Digest registers of births, marriages and burials for the General Meeting of Herefordshire, Worcestershire and Wales, 1635-1838 (mf) (D/D SF)

CHAPEL MEMORIAL INSCRIPTIONS

Memorial inscriptions from the following chapels: Caersalem, Aberbargoed; Saron and Hendy Cwrdd, Aberdare; Addoldy Independent; Alltwen Independent; Hepzibah, Bedwas; Carmel and Zoar, Bonvilston; Zoar, Smyrna, Ruhamah, Tabernacle and Newcastle Hill Unitarian, Bridgend; Betharan, Brynmenyn; Philadelphia, Cadoxton-juxta-Barry; Tonyfelin and Watford, Caerphilly; Tabernacle, the Hayes, Cardiff; Nebo, Cefn Cribbwr; Carmel and Hen-dy-Cwrdd, Cefn-Coed-y-Cymmer; Salem, Church Village; Bethania and Hebron, Clydach; Craig Penllyn Presbyterian; Tabernacle, Efail Isaf; Bethesda'r Fro, Eglwys Brewis; Gower Calvinistic Methodist chapels; Groeswen Congregational; Cefn Hengoed, Hengoed; Capel Rhondda and Pisgah, Hopkinstown; Pisgah, Kenfig Hill; Siloam, Killay; Providence, Knelston; Bethel, Laleston; Lisvane Baptist; Maendy, Llanblethian; Baran, Llangyfelach; Bethlehem, Llanharan; Peniel, Llanharry; Bryntirion and Salem, Llantwit Fardre; Beth, Ebenezer and Tabernacle, Llantwit Major; Old Zoar and Tabor, Maesycwmmer; Caepantywyll, Capel Bethlehem and Ebenezer, Merthyr Tydfil; Bethel, Morganstown; Salem, Nantyffyllon; Ebeneser, Nelson; Salem, Pencoed; Bethania, Pendoylan; Bronllwyn, Horeb and Penvel, Pentyrch; Capel Soar, Pen-y-graig; Croes-y-Parc, Peterston-super-Ely; Bethlehem, Peterston-super-Montem, Sardis, Pontypridd; Cymmer, Porth; Capel-y-Pil, Pyle; Soar, Rhiwceiliog; Bethlehem, Rhydyfelin; Soar-y-Graig, Rhymney; Ebenezer, Rhymney Valley; Ebenezer, St Bride's-super-Ely; Bethania and Caersalem, St Mellon's; Babell, Cwmbwrla, Swansea; Crug Glas Calvinistic Methodist Chapel, Swansea; Ainon, Glyndwr Taff and Tabor, Taff's Well; Ainon and Capel-y-Ton, Tonyrefail; Saron, Treforest; Siloam, Trehafod; Carmel and Libanus, Treherbert; Zoar, Wenvoe; Ararat, Beulah and Rhiwbina, Whitchurch; Wick Baptist and Unitarian; Bethania, Ystrad Mynach; Nebo, Ystrad Rhondda (D/D MI and microfiche)

CHAPEL PHOTOGRAPHIC SURVEY

Photographic survey of chapels in West Glamorgan carried out from 1993 to 1996. There are generally two photographs of each chapel, one of the exterior and, where possible, one of the interior. Chapel buildings which were no longer used for worship but which were still standing were included in this survey. (D/D CPS)

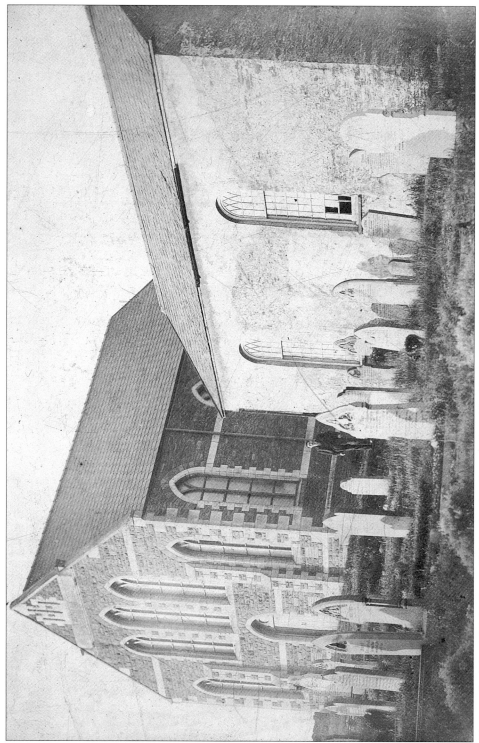

Photograph of Capel Triniti, Pontarddulais, showing the new chapel beside the old before demolition of the latter; circa 1891 (D/D W/Wes 72)

DONATIONS AND
DEPOSITS

DONATIONS AND DEPOSITS

Under the Local Government (Records) Act 1962, all county councils were empowered to accept local records by way of gift or loan from their owners, or to purchase them. This in fact regularised a practice which many county record offices had undertaken since their creation in the earlier years of this century. Nowadays, a large proportion of the archives held by the Archive Service are indeed donated or deposited, records of individuals or organisations which the owners have placed in the care of the Archive Service for safe-keeping and in order that they might be made available for research. Particularly of note is the acquisition of large estate collections, which are an invaluable resource for the study of local, and sometimes national, history.

This section of the Guide has been arranged by the subject matter of each collection. Individual items have also been listed outside the context of their collections, where they have a particular subject interest (note, however, that the archive reference number is still to the collection in which they may be found and not to the individual piece).

ABBEY CHARTERS

Two large monastic houses dominated the western part of Glamorgan- the abbeys of Neath and Margam. Neath Abbey was founded in 1129 and was originally a Savignac house, but soon became Cistercian: Margam was founded in 1147 as a daughter house of Clairvaux, also a Cistercian house. The Archive Service holds a charter from each of these abbeys.

Neath Abbey Charter (*circa* 1129)

The foundation charter of the Abbey, this records the gift of land and other property by Richard de Granville, Lord of Neath, and Constance his wife to the Abbey of the Holy Trinity at Savignac in Normandy in order to endow a new monastery which the Abbot of Savigny is to establish at Neath. There are seventeen witnesses. A declaration at the end in the name of the Earl of Gloucester takes all these matters under his patronage. Of the three original seals, only a parchment tag remains. (A/N 1)

Deed of gift to Neath Abbey (*circa* 1290)

Deed of gift to Neath Abbey from John Blanc Aignel relating to eight acres of land, probably in the manor of Penmaen, Gower, n.d. [*circa* 1290] (D/D Xge 103)

Margam Abbey Charter (1358)

This charter is one of a series of charters which recorded and confirmed the grants made by the Norman Lords of Glamorgan and Morgan to the Abbey of Margam. It dates from 1358. It is a long and complicated charter of confirmation recording an earlier charter of 1338, which had itself confirmed earlier charters from 1147 onwards. These are recited in the text. The grantor is Edward le Despenser, Lord of Glamorgan and Morgan, and nephew of Hugh le Despenser who had granted the charter of 1338. The wax seal, which only partly survives, is that of Edward le Despenser's Chancery at Cardiff and shows the Despenser coat of arms, with an equestrian portrait of Despenser brandishing a sword on the reverse. (A/Ma 1)

MANORIAL RECORDS

The manor was an area of land held by a landlord from the Crown either directly or indirectly, in a system known as feudal tenure. The tenants usually paid to the lord of the manor a mixture of money rents and goods or services, depending whether they were classed as villeins or freemen. The lord of the manor enforced the customs of the manor through courts baron and maintained law and order through courts leet.

The manor continued to exercise a role well into the modern age through the survival of copyhold as a form of land tenure. This was where the tenant's title was enrolled in manorial court records and an entry fine imposed by the court when the property passed from one copyholder to another. Copyhold tenure was abolished in 1922.

The custody of manorial documents is governed by the Manorial Documents Rules of 1959, 1963 and 1967. These rules are administered by the Royal Commission on Historical Manuscripts (HMC) on behalf of the Master of the Rolls. The County Hall repository is regularly inspected by the HMC and is an approved repository.

Seignory of Gower: Cromwellian survey, 1650 (18th century copy); survey of seignories of Gower and Kilvey by Gabriel Powell, 1764 (19th century copy); survey, *circa* 1821; notes on Gower manors, *circa* 1850 (D/D MG); manorial records for the manors of Cheriton, Horton, Kilvrough, Knelston, Landimore, Llangennith, Nicholaston, Oxwich, Penmaen, Pennard, Penrice, Pilton, Port Eynon, Reynoldston, Stembridge and Weobley, 1798-1939 (D/D P)

Manors of Neath (Neath Ultra and Cilybebyll, Neath Citra and Britton, Avon, Avon Wallia, Caegurwen and Tyr yr Allt): survey, 1728; extracts of fines and amerciments due, 1790-1794 (D/D MN); grant of lands in the lordship of Neath, 1400 (D/D Xgb); manorial records relating to manors of Avon, Avon Wallia, Neath, Neath Citra and Britton, Neath Ultra and Tyr yr Allt, 1726-1876 (D/D Gn)

Avon Wallia: presentment, 1711; notice to summon court, 1713 (D/D MN)

Bishopston: deeds, 1690-1814 (D/D Xfh), 1829-1866 (D/D X 288)

Caegurwen: court roll, 1688, 1690 and 1831-1925; minutes of general courts baron, 1903-1927; presentments, 1719, 1734-1901; legal records, 1720-1934; list of tenants, 1699, 1800 and 1914; lists of fines and amerciments, 1751-1768; extracts of chief rents, 1830, 1871 and 1888; admissions and surrenders, 1736-1841, 1915-1924 (D/D MN)

Ewenny: conveyance, 1710 (D/D MG)

Llangennith East Town (Priorstown): court book, 1821-1838 (SL)

Llangennith West Town: rentals, 1625-1660, including list of freeholders in Llangennith, 1650s (D/D Xgc)

Neath Citra and Britton: presentments, 1699-1718; appointment of Gabriel Powell as attorney to Thomas Mansel, 1705 (D/D MN)

Neath Ultra and Cilybebyll: court rolls, 1839-1935; presentments, 1687, 1701-1714, 1817; surrenders, 1614-1727; lists of tenants, 1654 (18th century copy), 1904 and 1914; lists of chief rents, 1779, 1811; admissions, 1915-1919, 1924-1925 (D/D MN)

Oystermouth and Pennard: court roll, admissions and surrenders, 1662-1676 (D/D MG); deeds, 1920 and 1923 (D152)

Pennard: court book, 1673-1701; part of court roll, 1685-1688; lists of admissions and surrenders, 1663, 1677, 1684; survey, 1650 (D/D MG); extract from court baron roll, 1817 (D/D Z 119); transcript of court book, 1673-1701 (D/D Z 177)

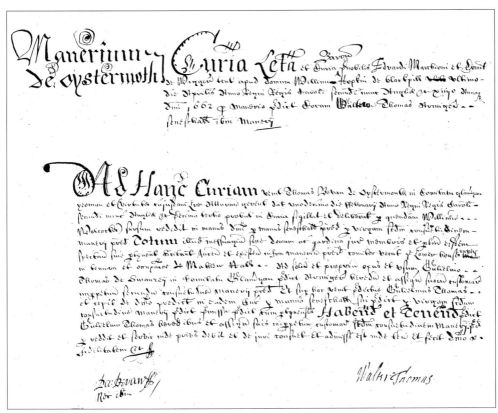

Court roll for the leet court of the Manor of Oystermouth, 1662 (D/D MG 2)

ESTATE AND FAMILY RECORDS

As in many other county record offices, estate records form an important part of the collections held by the Archive Service. They often contain material of both local and national interest, in that some of the great landowning families of Glamorgan were also involved in national politics. Other estate collections reflect the changes of the late nineteenth century and the rise of a new class of industrialist landowner based on the wealth of the South Wales coalfield.

The main estate collections are listed first, followed by collections of family and personal papers. Since many estate records form part of solicitors' collections, see also the section *Solicitors' Records* below.

Aberpergwm Estate

Williams family. Estate in the parish of Cadoxton-juxta-Neath.

Personal papers of Williams family, 1804-1919; architect's plans for Aberpergwm House, 1843, and papers relating to restoration and maintenance work on Aberpergwm House and garden, 1876-1920; title deeds and other legal documents, 1871-1915; accounts, 1848-1928; correspondence, 1867-1926; miscellaneous administrative papers, 1841-1920; diary (xerox) of trips to Continent by Morgan Stuart Williams, 1905-1909 (D/D Ab); journal of a visit to Italy by Morgan S Williams, 1899 (D/D Z 128); cash book, 1874-1875 (D/D Z 280); plans of private yachts of Godfrey Williams, 1910-1920 (D/D Z 253)

Part of this collection is held at the National Library of Wales. Records of the Williams' other Glamorgan estate, Castellau and St Donat's, are held at the Glamorgan Record Office, Cardiff.

Beaufort Estate

Surveys of the estate, 1803 and 1830 (D/D Beau); private Act concerning the Duke of Beaufort's family settlements and industrial leases, 1837 (D/D Z 223)

Briton Ferry Estate

The Briton Ferry Estate formed part of the lands of Margam Abbey and passed successively to the Mansel, Villiers and Vernon families (Earls of Jersey). The estate lay in the parishes of Aberavon, Baglan, Briton Ferry, Cadoxton-juxta-Neath, Glyncorrwg, Llangyfelach, Llansamlet, Llantwit-juxta-Neath, Margam, Michaelston-super-Avon, Neath, St John-juxta-Swansea, Swansea St Mary and Swansea St Thomas

Title deeds, 1679-1954; Cwmavon Building Estate underleases, 1897-1898 (D/D BF); rentals, 1823-1960; accounts, 1822-1937; lease books, 1813-1853; register of sales off, 1915-1951; correspondence, 1769-1866, 1891-1952; wills and related papers, 1783-1837; other legal papers, 1851-1895; estate plans and surveys including: survey of the Briton Ferry estate, *circa* 1780; survey and valuation of the estate, *circa* 1813; sale catalogues, 1818; plans of the estate, 1776-1913; other plans, 1899-1951; papers relating to the Briton Ferry Floating Dock, 1805-1930, including plans; papers relating to Neath Harbour, 1782-1886; papers relating to the Swansea Bay Graving Dock Company, 1884; papers relating to the Rhondda and Swansea Bay Railway Company, 1890-1908, including plans; papers relating to the Cwmavon Building Estate, 1897-1931; material relating to tithe, *circa* 1951 (D/D BF/E); lease register, 1940-1946 (D/D Z 20); pre-nuptial settlement, 1757, and abstract of title, 1815 (D/D Z 24)

There are a small number of Briton Ferry Estate deeds and related records, 1738-1856, in the Gnoll Estate collection (see *Gnoll Estate* below).

Calland (Upper Forest) Estate

Lands in the parish of Llangyfelach and Llansamlet.

Deeds, 1740-1939; schedules and plans, 1901-1903 (D218); deeds, 1850-1964 (D/D Xge); private Act, 1842 (D/D Xsa and D/D Z 137)

Cilybebyll Estate

Herbert and Lloyd families. Estates lying in the parishes of Cadoxton-juxta-Neath, Cilybebyll, Llangiwg, Llangyfelach (Glamorgan) and Llandeilofawr and Llangadog (Carmarthenshire)

Title deeds, 1497-1946; deeds of settlement, 1575-1954; mortgages, 1859-1916; survey and valuation, 1889; sale catalogue, 1916; plan of land to be acquired for a light railway from Morriston to Pontardawe, n.d. (D/D Cil); plan and correspondence, 1800-1838 (D/D Xga); estate accounts, 1819-1833 (D/D Xjl); correspondence, 1943-1953 (D/D SB 5)

Cwrt Ceidrim Estate

Estates principally in Llandeilo Talybont, Llangyfelach and Loughor, also in Carmarthenshire.

Deeds, 1659-1939 (D/D Xlf)

Dillwyn Estate

Lands in the parishes of Llangyfelach, Swansea, Oystermouth and in the Vale of Glamorgan.

Plans, 1922-1934 (D/D Xge)

Drumau Estate

Lands in the parishes of Llansamlet and Cadoxton-juxta-Neath.

Estate plans, 1777-1884; pedigrees of the Zacharia, Hopkins, Popkins and Thomas families, 1836-1906 (D/D Xdh)

Eaglesbush Estate

Families of Evans and Rice-Evans. Estates in the parishes of Coity, Llandeilo Talybont, Llansamlet, Llantwit-juxta-Neath and Neath, also lands in Monmouthshire.

Title deeds and other legal documents, 1589-1952; schedule of deeds and documents, after 1891; wills, 1726-1894; accounts, 1688-1892; correspondence, 1775-1846; family history notes on descendants of William ap Walter Thomas of Dan-y-Graig, *circa* 1840; family tree of the Pendrill, Pendrell or Penderel family, after 1922; volume containing a miscellany of legal opinions and notes, largely concerning the Mansell family, *circa* 1640-1708; translation of the Neath Abbey Charter, 1859; appointment of John, Earl of Bridgwater as Lieutenant for Wales, Monmouthshire, Herefordshire, Worcestershire and Shropshire, 1631; appointment of Henry, Marquis of Worcester as Lieutenant for North and South Wales, 1672; appointment of Deputy Lieutenants, 1674-1796; printed material, 18th-19th centuries; terrier, 1771; estate maps and plans, 1771-1899, including a map of the estate, 1837, and a plan of Eaglesbush Colliery subsequent to a mining disaster, 1900; canal and railway plans, 1792-1952 (D/D RE); estate plan, *circa* 1850 (D/D X 52); estate plan, *circa* 1882; report on the Eaglesbush Collieries, 1875; unlisted material (D/D TH)

Glasbrook Estate

John Glasbrook was a successful colliery owner who acquired land on the Glamorgan/Carmarthenshire border

Title deeds and other legal documents, 1859-1950 (D/D Gb)

Other papers of the Glasbrook family are in the Strick and Bellingham Collection. See under *Solicitors' Records* below.

Gnoll Estate

Evans, Mackworth, Leigh, Grant, Bushby and Evan-Thomas families. Estates lying mainly in the parishes of Aberavon, Baglan, Llangynwyd, Llantwit-juxta-Neath and Neath, and also properties in the counties of Brecon, Carmarthen, Montgomery and Radnor

Title deeds, 1606-1913 (D/D Gn); manorial records relating to manors of Avon, Avon Wallia, Neath, Neath Citra and Britton, Neath Ultra and Tyr yr Allt, 1726-1876; plans 1741-1882, including a plan of the Gnoll demesne by B Jones, *circa* 1741-1768, and an estate survey volume, 1855-1856 (D/D Gn/E); records of shipwrecks, 1778-1910; records of industrial undertakings, railways and other public utilities in Aberavon, Briton Ferry and Neath, 19th century (D/D Gn/I); estate plan, *circa* 1900 (D/D Xcx)

There are a small number of Briton Ferry Estate deeds and related records, 1738-1856, in this collection (see also *Briton Ferry Estate* above).

Gwyn Estate

Gwyn and Moore-Gwyn families. Estates lying in the parishes of Cadoxton-juxta-Neath, Cilybebyll, Llandeilo Talybont, Llangyfelach, Llangynwyd, Llansamlet and Neath, also lands in Breconshire, Carmarthenshire and Devon

Title deeds, 1667-1919; deeds of churches and schools, 1832-1944; mineral leases, 1806-1921, including a bundle relating to the Western Merthyr and Graigola Merthyr Colliery Companies, 1866-1920; sale catalogues, *circa* 1878-1949; estate plans, 1744-1845; property plans, 1883-1915; colliery plans, 1870-1920; railway plans, 1870-1921 (D/D Gw and D/D Gw/E)

Jenkins Estate

Elias Jenkins of Kilvey, Swansea (1779-1850) owned property in Glamorgan and Breconshire, including land in the parishes of Cadoxton-juxta-Neath, Cilybebyll, Llandeilo Talybont, Llangan, Llansamlet, Llantrisant, Llantwit-juxta-Neath, Merthyr Tydfil, Michaelston-super-Avon, Neath, St John-juxta-Swansea, Swansea St Mary, Swansea St Thomas and Penderyn (Breconshire)

Title deeds, 1666-1908; marriage settlements, wills and other legal records, 1732-1881; plans, mostly of farms, 1800-1901 (D/D Je)

Kilvrough Estate

Lyons family. Estates in the parishes of Ilston, Llangyfelach, Penmaen and Pennard

Title deeds, 1697-1937; Cromwellian survey of Gower, 1650 (copy made after 1832); accounts, 1847-1942; correspondence, 1915-1936; wages records, 1919-1922; sale catalogues, 1914-1932; farm records, 1904-1920; household accounts, 1859-1881; photographs, *circa* 1920 (D/D K); documents relating to sale of part of the estate, 1914-1935 (D/D Xtr); sale catalogues, 1918, 1919 (D/D Z 21) and 1920 (D/D Z 127)

Llewellyn of Baglan Hall and Cwrt Colman

History, 1989 (D/D Llew); estate plan, *circa* 1860 (D/D X 52); measured drawing of Baglan Hall, 1958 (D/D Z 261)

The main part of this collection is held at the Glamorgan Record Office, Cardiff.

Mansel Estate

Estates in Swansea, Carmarthenshire and elsewhere

Papers, 19th-20th centuries (D4); rent roll, *circa* 1831-1864; records, 1873-1929 (D/D Xge)

Margam Estate

Mansel and Talbot families. Estates lying mainly in the parishes of Aberavon, Kenfig, Laleston, Llandyfodwg, Llangeinor, Llangynwyd, Margam, Michaelston-super-Avon, Newton Nottage, St Bride's Major and Tythegston. Talbot family also owned the Penrice Estate (see below).

Margam Abbey Charter, 1358 (A/Ma 1); rentals and accounts, 1682-1940; cash books, 1784-1872; wages books, 1843-1891; household accounts, 1845-1932; poll books for Glamorgan election, 1820; ship's log book, 1806-1808; printed material relating to maritime affairs, 19th century; correspondence addressed to Christopher Rice Mansel Talbot, Lord Lieutenant of Glamorgan, 1889; Margam Home Farm accounts, 1906-1908; tithe records, including estate copies of tithe plans and apportionments; sale catalogues for parts of the estate, 1942 (D/D Ma); survey of the Margam estate by R W Hall, 1814 (D/D Ma/E); rentals, 1751-1757; accounts, 1743-1880 (including Penrice Estate); plan of proposed orangery at Margam, *circa* 1785 (D/D P); sale catalogue, 1917 (D/D Xgz); sale catalogue, 1941 (D/D Xgc); sale catalogue, 1960 (D/D Z 56); ship's logs for the Talbot family yachts, 1845-1873 (D/D Z 24); gamekeeper's diary, 1865; miscellanea, 1702-1991 (D/D Z 25)

There is related material at the National Library of Wales (Penrice and Margam Collection)

Morris Estate

Records, including papers concerning Sketty Park House 1845-1852, 19th-20th centuries (D11)

Neath Abbey Estate

Hoby family, Rice/Rhys of Dynevor (Lords Dynevor). Estates lying mainly in Cadoxton-juxta-Neath parish

54

Hopkin Llewellyn in his Account for Margam Estate with Thomas Mansel Talbot Esq[r].
By Cash paid towards building the NEW GREEN-HOUSE at Margam from the
24th day of March 1707 exclusive to the 24th day of March 1708 inclusive ———— Creditor

1707				
April 23	1	By what then paid William Gubbings on acco[t] of raising & working the Freestone in Pyle Quarrey for the New greenhouse at Margam as p[r] Receipt	30	
	2	By paid John Snook to the use of sev[l] Persons for Labouring Work done in digging part of the Foundation of the new Green-House, taking down the Garden Walls, wheeling Stones &c. towards the same in March last as p[r] Note thereof and Receipt appear	2	7
May 1	3	By paid W[m] Harry in full for 230 Crannocks of Lime towards Building the new Green-House at Margam as p[r] Note and Receipt appear	11	10
7	4	By p[d] Jn[o] Snook to the use of several Persons for sundry Labouring Work done in digging Earth for Morter, Repairing the Road to hale the Freestone from Pyle Quarrey, wheeling Stones & Rubbish and other Jobbs towards carrying on the Building of the New Green-House as p[r] Ditto	14	1 2
	5	By paid ditto to the use of Edw[d] Lewis & William Evan for Carpenters Work done at sundry Jobbs towards carrying on the Building of the new green House at Margam in April last as p[r] Note of Particulars thereof appear	2	17
	6	By paid William Gubbings on acco[t] to carry on the Building of the new greenhouse at Margam as p[r] Receipt	20	
14	7	By p[d] John Snook to the use of several Persons for Labouring Work done in digging Sand for Morter, wheeling Stones & Rubbish & other Jobbs towards carrying on the Building of the above greenhouse from the 26th day of April last exclusive to the 12th Instant inclusive as p[r] Note thereof and Receipt appear	10	16
25	8	By paid William Gubbings on Account of Building the new green House at Margam as p[r] Receipt appear	30	
28	9	By paid John Snook to the use of several persons for Labouring work done in digging Earth for Morter, wheeling Stones & Rubbish & other Jobbs towards forwarding the Building of the new Green house at Margam from the 12th to the 26th Instant inclusive as p[r] Note of Particulars appear	8	6
	10	By paid ditto to the use of William Evan & Edw[d] Lewis for Carpenters Work done in making wheelbarrows &c. Handbarrows, and various other Jobbs on acco[t] of the above Building from ditto to ditto as p[r] Ditto	2	4
June 11	11	By paid Ditto to the use of several persons for carpenters Work done in cutting and hubbling Scaffold Poles for the new Greenhouse at Margam, and also for Labouring Work done in digging Earth for Morter, wheeling Stones & Rubbish, & other Jobbs done towards carrying on the Same from 26th May last to the 11th Instant inclusive as p[r] Note and Receipt appear	11	9
	12	By paid Ditto to the Same use for digging part of the Foundation of ditto, & also for taking down the little Greenhouse as p[r] Ditto	7	1 4
	13	By paid William Harry for 237 Crannocks of Lime for the new greenhouse at Margam as p[r] Note and Receipt appear	11	17
July 2	14	By p[d] Jn[o] Snook to the use of several persons for Labour Work done in digging Earth for Morter, wheeling Stones & Rubbish, and sundry other Jobbs towards carrying on the Build[g] of the new greenhouse at Margam from the 11th to the 30th of June last inclusive as p[r] Note and Receipt appear	12	15 6
			£175 4	

Page from a Margam Estate account book showing expenditure on the building of Margam Orangery, 1788-1789 (D/D Ma 37)

Title deeds, 1668-1935; rentals and accounts, 1786-1944; wills of the Rice family, 1779-1845 (D/D D); sale catalogues of parts of the estate, 1837-1838; correspondence concerning damage to property from mine workings of Raven Colliery, Garnant; plans, 1770-1871, including a one-volume survey of the Neath Abbey Estate by John Davies, 1770-71, and a volume of plans of the Neath Canal, 1797-1892 (D/D D/E); sale catalogue, 1946 (D/D X 8); plan, 1799 (D/D SB 7)

Penrice Estate

Mansel and Talbot families. Estates lying mainly in the parishes of Nicholaston, Oxwich, Pennard, Penrice, Port Eynon, Reynoldston and Rhossili (the Gower Peninsula). The Talbot family possessed other estates based around the other family home at Margam (see *Margam Estate* above).

Title deeds, 1724-1923; correspondence, 1845-1900; rentals, 1751-1757 (including Margam Estate) and 1825-1913; accounts, 1743-1899 (some including Margam Estate); arrears book, 1724-1743; land and window tax assessments for Newcastle Hundred, 1704-1710; tenants' petitions, 1755; tithe records, 1857-1899; farm accounts, 1844-1906, including game records, labour books and building repair records; manorial records for the manors of Cheriton, Horton, Kilvrough, Knelston, Landimore, Llangennith, Nicholaston, Oxwich, Penmaen, Pennard, Penrice, Pilton, Port Eynon, Reynoldston, Stembridge and Weobley, 1798-1939; correspondence concerning coastguard houses at Rhossili, 1890-1892; Oxwich, Penrice and Port Eynon School Board accounts, 1882-1906; surveys of the estate, 1814 and 1831; estate maps by John Williams of parishes of Bishopston, Llanddewi, Llangennith and Knelston, Llanmadoc and Cheriton, Llanrhidian, Loughor, Nicholaston, Oxwich, Oystermouth, Pennard, Penrice, Port Eynon, Reynoldston, and Rhossili, 1780-1786; estate copies of tithe plans and apportionments; Swansea Local Board of Health plans, 1852; industrial plans relating to copper works and colliery at Penclawdd, 1840-1856; plans for the Gower Light Railway, 1896; photograph album, *circa* 1850; other material (unlisted) (D/D P); rentals, 1768-1781, 1843-1855 (D/D Ma)

There is related material at the National Library of Wales (Penrice and Margam Collection)

Tennant Estate

Tennant family. Estates lying in the parishes of Cadoxton-juxta-Neath, Cilybebyll, Llansamlet, Llantwit-juxta-Neath, Neath and Swansea

Title deeds, 1751-1913; rentals, 1814-1919; accounts, 1819-1938; tithe records, 1845-1924; estate correspondence, 1840-1920; records of industrial undertakings including canals, collieries, copperworks and quarries, 19th and 20th centuries; estate notebooks, 1815-1919, including much information on the estate's potential for industrial development; family papers and personal correspondence, including papers of the following: George Tennant (1765-1832); Gertrude Tennant (1820-1918); Jeremiah Richardson (1822-1906); George Pearce Serocold (1828-1912); Sir Henry Morton Stanley (1841-1904), the famous African explorer; Alice Tennant (1848-1930); Charles Coombe-Tennant (1852-1928); Dorothy Tennant (1855-1926); Winifred Coombe-Tennant (1874-1956) (D/D T); sale catalogue, 1872 (D/D X 88); sale catalogue, 1919 (D/D Xcx); measured drawing of Cadoxton Lodge, 1945 (D/D Z 261)

Twynboli Farm

Deeds and documents relating to Twynboli Farm, Llandeilofawr (Carmarthenshire), 1796-1869 (D/D Tw)

Vivian family

Personal papers and business records of Arthur Glendarves Vivian and other members of the Vivian family, 1851-1921; correspondence and reports concerning Morfa Colliery, 1886-1909; election papers, 1889-1892; correspondence and plan relating to the Hafod Schools and Swansea School Board, 1898 (D/D GV)

Whitworth Mineral Estates

The Whitworths were English gentry involved in mineral exploitation in the parishes of Baglan, Eglwysilan, Glyncorrwg, Llantwit-juxta-Neath and Michaelston-super-Avon.

Leases, 1728-1988, and other records, 1890-1951 (D/D WME); plans, 1858-1921; deeds, 1856-1930 (D/D Xra)

Ynyscedwyn Estate

Franklen, Aubrey, Portrey and Gough families. Estates lying in the parishes of Cadoxton-juxta-Neath, Cheriton, Cilybebyll and Llangiwg, also in the parishes of Brecon, Defynnog, Glyntawe, Talachddu, Ystradfellte and Ystradgynlais (Breconshire), Llanddeusant and Llandeilofawr (Carmarthenshire), Abergavenny, Goetre and Llanelen (Monmouthshire).

Title deeds of properties, including Gough family property in Gloucestershire, 1489-1945; sale catalogues, 1866-1935; industrial records, including records relating to Ynyscedwyn furnaces, 1801-1875, Ynyscedwyn Tin Plate Works, 1891-1925, Crane Foundry, Ystradgynlais, 1898-1922, miscellaneous collieries, 1808-1927, Gurnos Brick and Tinplate Works, 1877-1920, Tirbach Brick Works, 1890-1904; wills, 1891-1904; estate plans, 1797-1934, including surveys by John Williams, 1797, and Philip Thomas, 1838; Ystradgynlais National School and other educational records, 1773-1816; personal papers and correspondence, 18th-20th centuries (D/D Yc); sale catalogues, 1920-1924 (D/D Xcx)

Ynyspenllwch Estate

Miers family. Estates in the parishes of Cadoxton-juxta-Neath, Llangiwg and Llangyfelach

Mortgages, wills and settlements, 1801-1914; leases and building agreements, 1840-1937; mineral leases, 1867-1926; register of leases, 1860s-1920s; rentals, 1893-1965; accounts, 1939-1966; sale catalogues, 1894-1895; copies of local railway Acts, 1911-1912; estate plans, 1862-1900; GWR plans, 1911-1912; plans of Ynyspenllwch House, *circa* 1900; survey of the Edmondes (Old Hall) Mineral Estate, Upper Rhondda, 1929; correspondence and papers from the Ynyscedwyn Estate, 1892-1912 (D/D Yp); sale catalogue, 1914 (D/D Xcx)

Miscellaneous

Sale catalogues for the following estates: Dyffryn Estate, 1873-1927; Rheola Estate, 1920; Ynystawe Estate, 1917; also Brunant, Cawdor, Craig-y-Nos, Nantgwynne and Stouthall (D/D Xcx); Baglan Estate, 1919 (D/D Xlm); Bronwydd Estate, 1948 (D/D Xrm); Summerland Estate, 1930 (D/D Z 16); Pentrepoeth Estate, 1919 (D225); sale particulars of property and estates in Swansea, 1783-1920 (SL)

Family and personal papers

Alfred Baglow of Mumbles: personal papers of former gold miner in British Columbia and soldier in Canadian Expeditionary Force during First World War, 1913-1922 (D223)

Eileen Baker of Gurnos: autobiography of a 1920s childhood, 1992 (D/D Z 136)

Captain John Bevan of Mumbles: personal papers and photographs, 19th-20th centuries (D/D Z 141)

Sir Arthur Whitten Brown: notes on and photographs of the pioneering air navigator, 1930s-1980s (D/D Z 21)

Elizabeth Charles of Pontrhydyfen: travel diary while on tour with Madam Hughes Thomas' Ladies Choir, 1911-1912 (D/D Z 13)

Coulthard, Rogers and Davies families of Oystermouth: family tree, *circa* 1800-1981 (D/D Z 27)

Cox family of Swansea: family tree, 1843-1990 (D/D Z 30)

David family of Llangynwyd: legal papers of David family of Forest Nant Herbert Farm, Llangynwyd and Glyncorrwg, 1772-1940 (D/D Z 269)

David/Davies family of Seven Sisters: farmers at Ynysdawley, diaries, 1826-1928 (D/D Xjx)

George Sydney Davies of Swansea: diary, 1866-1879 (D/D Z 334)

Captain H Leighton Davies (1894-1980) of Swansea: family and business papers, 1908-1974 (D/D Z 53)

W J Davies of Morriston: papers relating to adult education in Swansea, 1919-1952 (SL WJD)

Forsdike family of Llanelli: family history of Forsdikes in Llanelli and rest of Wales, 1840-1995 (D/D Z 239)

Gammon family of Oystermouth: papers, 1794-1984 (D/D Xgc)

Gilbertson of Pontardawe: notes on the family and Company, 1944-1966 (D/D X 93)

Glasbrooke family of Llangyfelach: family history, 1992 (D/D Z 149)

Griffiths family of Rhossili: family tree, 1520-1995 (D/D Z 242)

Griffiths family of West Glamorgan: family tree, 1700-1969 (D/D Z 323)

Hancorne family of Glamorgan: family tree, 17th-20th centuries, 1995 (D/D Z 221)

B Harmer: unpublished autobiography including recollections of childhood in Mumbles orphanage, n.d. (D150)

Hayman family of Somerset, Devon, Kent and South Wales: family trees, 1037-1867 (D/D Z 46)

M Hemmings of Swansea: diary of Miss M Hemmings, 1918 (D/D X 192)

Heneage-Vivian family of Swansea: papers, 1915-1918 (D1)

Hosgood family of Neath: papers, 1794-1984 (D/D Xgc)

Edward Hughes of Swansea: personal papers, *circa* 1750-1800 (SL EH)

Jeffreys family of Swansea: family history, 17th-20th centuries, 1992-1997 (D/D Z 167)

Emrys Jenkins of Ystalyfera: diary of First World War sailor, 1916-1919 (D/D Z 249)

Jenkins family of Manselfold, Gower: family history, *circa* 1992 (D/D Z 149)

Jenkins, Jones and Morgan families of Llandeilo Talybont: family history, 1993 (D/D Z 149)

J R Jones of Seven Sisters: family papers, *circa* 1900-1940 (D/D Z 72)

Emile Knecht (French Vice Consul at Swansea): correspondence and photographs, 1887-1902 (D75, *restricted access*: only by prior written permission from the County Archivist)

Ivor Laugharne of Grovesend: papers, 1920s-1970s (D/D X 192)

Llewelyn of Penllergaer: family tree, *circa* 1950 (D/D Z 21)

Llewhelling family of Loughor and Swansea: family and business papers, 1760-1863 (D/D Z 46)

W W Loxton: autobiographical work, *The Swansea I Remember*, 1950s (D200)

William Mansel of Swansea: correspondence, 1897-1903; travel diary, *circa* 1900; election ephemera, 19th century (SL WM)

H Grindell Matthews, inventor, of Llangyfelach: newscuttings, photographs and manuscript biography, 1910-1994 (D/D Z 346)

Morgan family, farmers, of Ystradgynlais: deeds and documents, 1726-1940, including a notebook containing folk medecine and husbandry advice, 1726-1768 (D/D Z 123)

Pendrill, Pendrell or Penderell family: family tree, 1660-1922 (D/D RE)

D Rhys Phillips of Swansea: papers of and collected by the former Swansea librarian and author, 19th century, including papers relating to Unitarians in South Wales (SL DRP)

Prust family of Swansea: family tree, 1805-1987 (D/D Z 251)

Rees of Sketty Hall, Swansea: papers relating to the tenancy of the Hall and miscellaneous records including photographs, *circa* 1870 (D/D Z 97)

Rice family of Carregllwyd, Llangyfelach: family papers, 1831-1955 (D/D Z 28)

Riddero family of Gower: family tree, 1728-1965 (D/D Z 26)

Savours family: pedigree, n.d. (D46)

Reverend Thomas Sims (1785-1864) of Llansamlet: notes on this scholar of Protestant church history, 1995 (D/D Z 259) .

Susanna Staniforth: *Remembrances of Swansea Bay*, 1840 (D/D Z 62)

T E Stradling: history of Lonlas and Llwynbrwydrau and notes on the Stradling family, 1997 (D/D Z 338)

Idris Thomas of Morriston: a collection of facsimiles relating to a disabled child who was received at Buckingham Palace, 1912 (D/D Z 298)

Reverend Thomas William Walters of Kilvey: papers, 1893-1904 (D179)

Webborn and Lewis families: deeds and other papers, 1801-1885 (D93)

Bernard Whelan of Swansea: war diary, 1939-1945 (D229)

Sally Young of Bristol: journals, 1798-1805 (D/D Z 24)

William Weston Young (1776-1847) of Bristol, Aberdulais and Neath: diaries, 1801-1843 (D/D Xch); diaries and plans, 1787-1840 (D/D Xhf); diary, 1807 (D/D Xls)

Photographs of David Lloyd George with the Coombe-Tennant family at Cadoxton, 1923 (D/D T 4166 and 4167)

SOLICITORS' RECORDS

T R Harris Arnold & Company, solicitors, Swansea

Deeds of properties in Swansea, 19th-20th centuries (D12)

Collins, Woods and Vaughan Jones, solicitors, Swansea

Hodgens family of Swansea: personal papers and photographs, 1888-1988 (D/D CV 3)

Lewis family of Gorseinon: deeds and legal papers, *circa* 1820-1950. Includes some business records of Cross Foundry, Gorseinon, 1881-1908, and Grovesend Steel and Tinplate Company, 1909-1930 (D/D CV 4)

Deeds of properties in Swansea, 18th-20th centuries (D17)

Also unlisted material, including papers of the Heneage-Vivian family (D/D CV)

F H Edwards, solicitors, Swansea

Maps and plans, including deed and plans relating to the Crawshay Bailey Estate, 1865-1960 (D/D FHE)

Cyril Goldstone and Company, solicitors, Swansea

Miscellaneous title deeds, n.d. (D109)

Strick and Bellingham, solicitors, Swansea

General: letter books, 1929-1947; telegram books, 1915-1939; London agent's letter book, 1940-1947; general ledgers, 1910-1956; account books, 1892-1942; estate sale catalogues, 1885-1950; wills, letters of administration and grants of probate, 1828-1975 (D/D SB 1)

Port of Swansea: registers of protests of ship's masters before public notary, 1936-1979 (D/D SB 2)

Ynystawe Estate (Martin family): letter books, 1889-1948; deeds and leases, 1595-1935; rentals, 1890-1947; valuations, 1908, 1915; journals, 1896-1940; mineral royalty accounts, 1919-1942; account books, 1896-1948; index of leases granted, 1842-1921; estate plans, 1836-1933 (D/D SB 3)

Cilybebyll Estate (Lloyd family): correspondence, 1943-1953 (D/D SB 5)

Neath Abbey Estate: estate plan, 1799 (D/D SB 7)

Swansea and Mumbles Railway: legal records and associated correspondence, 1804-1953 (D/D SB 9)

Glanamman Colliery: plans, 1942 (D/D SB 11)

Benson family of Llanrhidian: deeds and associated records, 1827-1922 (D/D SB 12)

James family of Brynaman (Neuadd Estate): deeds, legal papers and correspondence, *circa* 1800-1950. Includes business records of the Amman Anthracite Collieries Ltd, the Amman Iron Company and the Birch Rock Colliery (D/D SB 13)

Richardson Estate (Swansea and Glanbrydan Park, Carmarthenshire): deeds and other estate records, 1776-1971 (D/D SB 14)

Glasbrook family of Swansea, colliery proprietors etc: business records and family papers, 1812-1988 (D/D SB 15)

Also unlisted material, including records of the Moore-Gwyn Estate (D/D SB)

David and Roy Thomas, solicitors, Mumbles

Deeds relating to properties on Wind Street, Swansea, 1870-1934 (D113)

Trethowan's, solicitors, Swansea: records (unsorted and unlisted) (D82)

John F Harvey and Sons, chartered accountants, Swansea: deeds of properties in South Wales, 1873-1939 (D/D JFH)

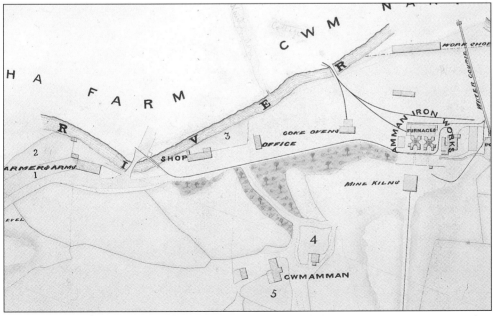

Detail from a volume of maps showing land and minerals belonging to the Amman Iron Company, Brynaman, 1857 (D/D SB 13 E/1)

ANTIQUARIAN COLLECTIONS

Rowland Morton Davies of Swansea (1908-1995)

Rowland (Rowley) Davies collected photographs of Swansea, including many slides which he used in public lectures after his retirement from the Estates Department of Swansea City Council. Part of his photograph collection formed the nucleus of the civic picture collection listed below in the section *Pictures and Photographs*.

Miscellaneous files of photographs, press cuttings, articles and correspondence, including files on the Blitz on Swansea, the Mumbles train, Swansea suburbs, and a series of articles written for the *South Wales Evening Post*, 1970s-1990s

Miscellaneous books and articles on the history of Swansea, 1875-1992

Slides arranged for lectures, n.d.; slides arranged by subject, n.d. (unlisted)

Sound recordings, n.d. (unlisted)

(D/D RMD)

Arthur Leslie Evans of Port Talbot (1911-1996)

Leslie Evans was an enthusiastic collector and prolific writer on the local history of his native Port Talbot. A schoolteacher by profession, he was also a gifted poet and artist, illustrating many of his own publications. He wrote numerous books, monographs and articles on the Port Talbot district. He was chairman of the Port Talbot Historical Society from 1958 until 1996, and editor of the Society's Transactions.

Published and unpublished writings: The administration of justice in the Port Talbot district in bygone days; Margam Abbey; Ordinance of the Borough of Afan; Sker House; the story of Taibach and district; the story of Baglan; The Globe, Aberavon; the parish church of St James, Pyle; Cae Dan y Graig, Margam; the lords of Afan; the mayors and portreeves of Aberavon and Port Talbot; smugglers, wrecks and pirates in the Bristol Channel; an untitled novel.

Notebooks on local history, various dates; newscutting books, 1880s-1990s; poetry, n.d.; copies of documents, including Kenfig Borough minutes, 1817-1853, and collected documents, including Margam Parish overseers' accounts, 1700-1800; sale catalogues 1860-1919; maps and plans, 1824-1994; correspondence, 1950s-1990s; postcards, pictures and photographs, various dates.

(D/D LE)

William Cyril Rogers of Swansea (1912-1995)

During long service in the Estates Department of Swansea County Borough then City Council, W C Rogers made extensive notes on the history and antiquities of his native Swansea and also of South Wales. He accumulated large quantities of notes, some of which were filed by subject. He also collected photographs of Swansea.

Chronological notes on national historical events, 1074-1979; chronological notes on local historical events, 1887-1974; topographical notes on places in Glamorgan, n.d.; topographical notes on places in the Lordship of Gower, n.d.; topographical notes on places in Carmarthenshire, Cardiganshire and Pembrokeshire, n.d.; notes on Swansea inns; notes on Gower placenames; transcripts of early Swansea charters, terriers, inventories and inquisitions, 16th-19th centuries; family history notes and genealogies; notes on Gower and Glamorgan families; index of Gower family names taken from the Carmarthen Probate Registry lists; alphabetical list of the hereditary burgesses of Swansea (incomplete); lists of mayors and other public officers of Swansea, all n.d.; other material (unlisted)

(D/D WCR)

Plans: volume of plans showing the ancient and modern boundaries of the Borough of Swansea, collected by George Grant Francis, 1853; folder of maps and plans of parts of Swansea (including modern copies), 1764-1881; loose plans of Swansea, including the harbour, Llangyfelach, and roads, railways and canals in Swansea and South Wales (mostly copies), 1641-1926 (D/D WCR/Pl)

Photographs of Swansea, various dates (D/D WCR and D37)

Gower Families Index

Other collections

Reverend Latimer Davies: Notes on and extracts of history and antiquities of Gower, n.d.; census of 20 Gower parishes of 1563, 19th century copy (D/D Xar)

LIBRARY AND MUSEUM COLLECTIONS

The library and museum collections listed below, those of the Neath, Port Talbot and Swansea Libraries and of Neath Museum, have all been transferred to the custody of the Archive Service.

Neath Library Collection (NL)

Municipal records

Borough of Neath: minutes, 1850-1890, 1921-1971; committee minutes, 1922-1968; Profiteering Committee minutes, 1919; councillors' declaration books, 1835-1910; poll record books, 1881-1914; Neath Gas Act, 1866; Gas Inspector's minute book, 1869-1886; Highway Board minutes, 1876-1880; Neath Joint Hospital Committee minutes, 1912-1939; Neath and District Tramways Company Ltd minutes, 1876-1885; Neath Local Benefit Society and Savings Band minutes, 1857-1885; Neath, Swansea and Aberavon Borough extension inquiry, 1920-1922; Neath Constabulary, correspondence (unlisted); Neath Education Board, correspondence (unlisted); correspondence on markets, public health and Neath Harbour (unlisted) (NL B/N)

Neath Burial Board: correspondence (unlisted) (NL Bu B/N)

Briton Ferry Local Board of Health: minutes, 1864-1874; draft minutes, 1864-1895; letter book, 1879-1880; Surveyor's letter book, 1876-1896; register of owners of property and their proxies, 1873-1879; accounts, 1881-1896 (NL L/B BF)

Briton Ferry Urban District Council: draft minutes, 1895-1908; letter books, 1898-1922; correspondence, 1890-1921 (unlisted); register of attendance of councillors, 1898-1916; register of motions, 1901; Sanitary Inspector's reports, 1896-1909; Engineer's and Surveyor's letter books, 1892-1896, 1902-1923; accounts, 1880-1885, 1903-1908; Engineer's ledger, 1893-1919; wages records, 1891-1903; planning registers, 1882-1908; registers of explosives, 1891-1920; register of petrol filling stations, 1912-1922; register of omnibus drivers and conductors, 1914-1920; register of cowkeepers and dairymen, 1920-1922; register of dairies, 1906-1922; rate abstracts, 1924-1925; accounts, 1897-1899 (NL UD/BF)

Briton Ferry Burial Board: register of burials and graves, 1880-1896; accounts, 1896-1907 (NL Bu B/BF)

Neath Rural District Council: minutes, 1894-1973; various committee minutes, 1895-1973 (NL RD/N)

Business records

Copies of local railway bills and associated correspondence: Brynaman and Neath Railway Bill, 1902; Briton Ferry Docks and Railway Act, 1851; Great Western Railway Bills, 1889,

1904 and 1911; Great Western Railway Neath River Crossing Bill, 1892; Neath, Pontardawe and Brynaman Railway Bills, 1895 and 1904; Rhondda and Swansea Bay Railway Bills, 1882-1895; South Wales Mineral Railway Bill, 1907; opposition to the Railway and Canal Traffic Act, 1888; miscellaneous other Local Railway Acts, 1845-1931; Neath Corporation Tramways Bill, 1897

E C Jones of Neath, architect: letter books, 1864-1921

Joshua Richardson of Neath, civil engineer: journal, 1841-1850

Neath Museum Collection (NM)

Borough of Neath: accounts, 1924-1972; rating records, 1876-1968; register of new dwellings, 1957-1962 (NM B/N)

Briton Ferry Urban District Council: rating records, 1900-1914 (NM UD/BF)

Neath Rural District Council: accounts, 1885-1982 (NM RD/N)

Port Talbot Library Collection (PTL)

Municipal records

Borough of Aberavon: minutes, 1861-1914; material concerning the legality of the Charter of Incorporation, *circa* 1861-1863; burgess roll, 1861-1882; register of enrolment, 1861-1880; poll book, 1867-1870; deeds, 1848-1921; correspondence, 1894-1910; rate books, 1912-1921; accounts, 1914-1917; Surveyor's Department plans, 1903-1919 (PTL B/A)

Borough of Port Talbot: committee reports and related material, 1902-1955; deeds, 1923-1938; registers of mortgages, 1867-1952; record of civilian war deaths, 1940-1941; registers of factories, 1938-1964; petroleum licences, 1951-1958; hackney carriage licences, 1950-1961; accounts, 1922-1960; Treasurer's letter books, 1944-1950; rating records, 1924-1963; cemetery records, 1945-1962; civil defence records, 1938-1942; Surveyor's records, 1950-1962; planning registers, 1937-1939; building regulation plans, 1923-1956; slum clearance plans, 1930-1938 (PTL B/PT)

Glyncorrwg Urban District Council: minutes, 1968-1974; building regulation plans, 1883-1947 (PTL UD/Gl)

Margam Urban District Council: minutes, 1896-1915; deeds and associated records, 1898-1921; accounts, 1912-1918; rating records, 1879-1924; Surveyor's records, 1919-1920 (PTL UD/Ma)

Neath Rural District Council: minutes, 1895; cemetery plan, 1915 (PTL RD/N)

Business records

Log book of the barque *Fidelity*, 1847-1848

Port Talbot Pilotage Authority: registers of pilotage and vessels in and out, 1895-1951; pilotage returns, 1913-1933; log books of pilot cutter *Marian Byass*, 1934-1952; bye-laws, 1924; letters out, 1904-1923; letters in, 1906-1923; accounts, 1936-1955 (PTL PTHa)

Port Talbot Pilotage Cutter Company: minutes, 1912-1934; register of towages, 1931-1934; accounts, 1912-1945 (PTL PTHa)

Records of societies

Aberavon and Port Talbot District Nursing Association: minutes, 1898-1959; miscellaneous items, 1899-1973 (PTL PTNA)

Baglan Rifle Range Association: plans and correspondence, 1909-1914

Bryn Billiard Club: receipt book, 1916-1940

Caradoc ap Iestyn Lodge of True Ivorites: minutes, 1864-1935

Gowerton Rifle Range Association: plans and correspondence, 1913-1918

Maesteg Drill Hall Association: plans and correspondence, 1912-1913

Royal Welsh Show, Port Talbot: minutes and associated correspondence, 1959

Welsh National Eisteddfod, Aberavon: list of competitors and winners, 1932

Swansea Library Collection

Municipal records

Glamorgan Roads Board: case papers, Swansea Improvements and Tramways Company *vs* County Roads Board for Glamorganshire, 1878-1880 (SL CRB)

Borough of Swansea: copy of Cromwellian charter, 1655; letter concerning the use of Velindre Pit as water supply, late 19th century; reports of the Swansea Gas Light Company, 1892-1909 (SL WM)

Cockett Parish: minutes, 1894-1914; correspondence, 1895-1917 (SL P/325)

Coedffranc Parish: minutes, 1868-1915 (SL P/71)

Llansamlet Parish: minutes, 1876-1914; tithe rentals, 1877-1881 (SL P/160)

Ecclesiastical records

Swansea St Jude (ecclesiastical parish): vestry minutes, 1892-1897; PCC minutes, 1919-1920; Sunday School records, 1902-1925 (SL P/320/CW)

Manorial records

Manor of East Town of Llangennith (Priorstown): court book, 1821-1838

Business records

John Bevan and Son, chemical manufacturers of Llanelli: accounts, 1890s-1936

The Cambrian **newspaper (William Mansel papers):** accounts and miscellanea, 1786-1889; articles of association of limited company, 1890-1899; company accounts, 1890-1896; correspondence, 1851-1912 (SL WM)

Rhondda and Swansea Bay Railway: miscellaneous records, 1880-1897

Swansea Theatre Tontine (William Mansel papers): minutes, 1855-1891; accounts, 1805-1891; list of subscribers, 1805; rules, 1875; legal papers, 1857-1882; correspondence, 1826-1889; history, 1878 (SL WM)

Records of societies

Association of Bookmen of Swansea and West Wales: constitution, *circa* 1943; minutes, 1943-1961; accounts, 1946-1964; correspondence, 1948-1962 (SL AB)

Swansea and District Federation of the Church of England Men's Society: constitution, 1922; minutes, 1910-1924; accounts, 1915-1923; correspondence, 1914-1923 (SL CE)

Swansea Gospel Mission: attendance registers, 1876-1900; journals and notebooks, 1864-1887; correspondence, 1872-1876 (SL GM)

Swansea and South West Wales District Society of Incorporated Accountants: minutes, 1932-1948

Personal papers

W J Davies of Morriston: papers relating to adult education in Swansea, 1919-1952 (SL WJD)

Edward Hughes of Swansea: personal papers, *circa* 1750-1800 (SL EH)

William Mansel of Swansea: correspondence, 1897-1903; travel diary, *circa* 1900; election ephemera, 19th century (SL WM)

D Rhys Phillips of Swansea: papers of and collected by the former Swansea librarian and author, 19th century, including papers relating to Unitarians in South Wales (SL DRP)

Miscellaneous: Wyld's plan of Swansea, late 19th century; ephemera relating to the opening of the Prince of Wales Dock, 1881 (SL WM); sale catalogues of property and estates in Swansea, 1783-1920; plan of Swansea Town, 1851; plan of line of intended Swansea Canal, n.d.

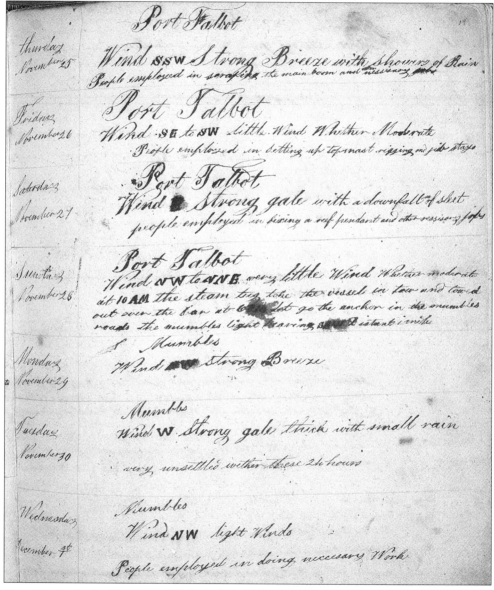

Part of the log book of the barque 'Fidelity' of Port Talbot, 1847 (PTL 1)

BUSINESS AND INDUSTRIAL RECORDS

Aluminium smelting

ICI Aluminium Works, Waunarlwydd: photograph album, *circa* 1940s (D101)

Architects

Jonah Arnold & Smith, architects, Neath: building plans, *circa* 1920-1970 (D/D JAS)

E C Jones, architect, Neath: letter books, 1864-1921 (NL)

Banking records

Bank of Wales: papers relating to the establishment of a Bank of Wales, 1853-1856 (D/D BW)

Breweries

List of inns, taverns and public houses in Swansea, 1876 (D214)

List of public houses in Swansea and Gower, 1900 (D/D Z 291)

Plans of Evans Bevan hotels in Port Talbot, n.d. (D40)

see also *Public Houses* below

Brick companies

Gurnos Brick and Tinplate Works: records, 1877-1920 (D/D Yc)

Tirbach Brick Works: records, 1890-1904 (D/D Yc)

Vale of Neath Dinas Fire-brick and Cement Co Ltd: records, 1860, *circa* 1921 (D/D X 177)

Builders and masons

Griffith Davies and Co Ltd, building contractors, Swansea: account books, 1932-1969 (D/D X 147)

J Jones, builders, Swansea: miscellaneous records, 19th-20th centuries (D230)

Roderick and Son, masonry craftsmen, Port Talbot: account books, 1896-1967 (D/D X 42)

D R Williams, building contractors, Pontardawe: accounts, 1913-1933 (D/D Z 65)

Canal companies

Neath Canal: Neath Canal Act, 1790 (D/D Xcf); minutes, 1791-1867; shareholders' records, 1830-1917; accounts, 1791-1924; correspondence, 1878-1895; legal papers, 1801-1906;

deeds, 1794-1896 (D/D NCa, *restricted access:* only by prior written permission from the County Archivist)

Swansea Canal: Swansea Canal Act, 1794, and associated papers (D/D Z 271); plan of line of intended Swansea Canal, n.d. (SL)

Tennant Canal: accounts, 1818-1916; legal papers, 1816-1919; correspondence, 1832-1927; unpublished history, 1919 (D/D T)

Car manufacturers

Ford Motor Company, Swansea: history of the Ford Motor Company site in Swansea, 1964-1967 (D/D Z 332)

Carpet retailers

Bailey Carpets of Swansea: accounts, 1914-1942 (D/D JFH)

Chemical manufacturers

John Bevan and Son, chemical manufacturers, Llanelli: accounts, 1890s-1936 (SL)

Chemists

J T Davies, Dispensing Chemists, Swansea: prescription books, 1877-1971 (D/D JTD)

Hibbert & Son, Pharmaceutical Chemists, Neath: prescription book, 1855-1864 (D/D Xln); prescription, 1909 (D/D Z 138)

S R Morris, Dispensing Chemists, Gowerton: prescription book, 1912-1926 (D/D Z 62)

Civil engineers

Joshua Richardson, civil engineer, Neath: journal, 1841-1850 (NL)

Collieries

Amman Anthracite Collieries Ltd: business records, 1930-1934 (D/D SB 13)

Birch Rock Colliery: business records, 1867-1881 (D/D SB 13)

Birchgrove Colliery: deeds, 1870-1922 (D/D Xge)

Blaencaegurwen Colliery: sale catalogue, 1931 (D/D Xcx)

Broadoak Colliery: plan, 1933 (D/D Z 24)

Bryn Newydd Colliery, Bryn: miscellaneous records, including correspondence files of the Small Mines Federation, 1960s-1980s (unlisted) (D/D Z 253)

Brynaman Minerals: leases, 1874-1898 (D/D Xkc)

Brynglas Colliery, Tairgwaith: records, 1964-1979 (D/D Z 253, *restricted access:* only by prior written permission from the County Archivist)

Cefnstylle Colliery: photograph, *circa* 1900 (D/D Z 188)

Clyne Valley Colliery: maps and plans relating to Clyne Valley and nearby collieries and other works, 1957-1981 (D/D Z 46)

Copper Pit Colliery, Morriston: survey of underground workings, 1922 (D123)

Craig Merthyr Colliery: photograph, *circa* 1915 (D/D Z 38)

Cwmavon and Oakwood Collieries: wages books, 1878-1881; other account books, 1874-1901 (D/D Xlm)

Cwmllynfell Colliery: miscellaneous report books and accounts, 1849-1878 (D/D Xef); lease, 1825 (D/D Xfd)

Cwmnantmoel Colliery Company: correspondence files, 1947-1969; plans, 1957-1974 (D/D Z 253)

Dyffryn Main Colliery Company: accounts, 1874 (D/D Xgb)

Eaglesbush Colliery: deeds, 1869-1874 (D/D Xge)

Emlyn Anthracite Colliery Ltd: memorandum and articles of association, 1939; accounts, 1959-1977 (D189)

Glanamman Colliery: plans, 1942 (D/D SB 11)

Glasbrook Collieries: business records and family papers, 1812-1988 (D/D SB 15)

Graig Merthyr Colliery, Pontarddulais: miscellaneous records, 1907-1930 (D/D Z 68)

Graigola Colliery: plans, 1919-1926 (D/D Xcx)

Killan Colliery: records (unsorted and unlisted) (D83)

Main Colliery Skewen: articles of association, 1889; minutes, 1889-1928; annual reports, 1890-1925; chairman's papers, 1900-1927; correspondence, 1889-1934; accounts, 1885-1930; share registers, 1889-1928; sales figures and output sheets, 1884-1928; receivership papers, 1928-1934; mining plans, n.d.; architectural and engineering plans, *circa* 1890-1926 (D/D MC); advertising brochure, *circa* 1899 (D/D Xgt); sale catalogue, 1930 (D/D Xcx and D/D Z 21); photographs, *circa* 1900 (D/D Z 240)

Morfa Colliery: correspondence and reports concerning Morfa Colliery, 1886-1909 (D/D GV); article and illustration, 1863 (D/D Xgb)

Mynydd Newydd Colliery, Swansea: plan, after 1868 (D/D Z 204)

Penclawdd Colliery: industrial plans relating to copper works and colliery at Penclawdd, 1840-1856 (D/D P)

Raven Colliery, Garnant: correspondence concerning damage to property from mine workings of Raven Colliery, Garnant (D/D D/E)

Tirffordd Colliery, Llangyfelach: photographs, n.d. (D/D Z 275)

Universal Colliery, Senghenydd: minutes of inquiry into colliery disaster, 1914 (D/D Z 192)

Whitworth Mineral Estates Company: leases, 1728-1988, and other records, 1890-1951 (D/D WME); prospectus and plan, 1905 (D/D Xki)

Ynyscedwyn Estate Collieries: records relating to miscellaneous collieries, 1808-1927 (D/D Yc); photograph, *circa* 1900 (D/D Z 33)

Miscellaneous: photographs taken above and below ground in small mines in the Neath and Dulais Valleys, 1990-1993 (D/D Z 175); plans of Gleision Colliery, Godre'rgraig, 1962, and Yniseu, Graig-y-Fforest and Brynvarteg Collieries, all undated (D/D Xqk).

Colliery records are also to be found listed in the section above *Other Public Records* under the headings *National Coal Board* and *Health and Safety Executive*.

Copper smelters

Governor and Company of Copper Miners in England, Cwmavon and Bryn Works: miscellaneous records, 1860-1873 (D/D Xnf)

English Copper Company: plan of copper works and lands at Margam, 1834 (D/D Xk)

John Freeman and Copper Company: deeds, correspondence and accounts, 1734-1884, including some items relating to White Rock Copper Works, Llansamlet, 1736-1854 (D/D Xhr)

Hafod Copper Works: history, 1905 (D/D Xgb); notes on the works and on other industrial sites in the Swansea Valley, 1830-1831 (D255)

Llanelly Copper Company: minute book, accounts and plans, 1861-1872 (D/D Xav)

Penclawdd Copper Works: industrial plans relating to copper works and colliery at Penclawdd, 1840-1856 (D/D P)

Yorkshire Imperial Metals: records of Landore Works, 1811-1944 (D34)

Miscellaneous: French article on the treatment of copper ore in South Wales, 1825 (D/D Z 270)

Dry dock companies

Port Talbot Dry Dock Company: records, 1898-1969 (D/D X 105)

Prince of Wales Dry Dock Company, Swansea: records, 1897-1971 (D/D X 105)

Electricity undertakings

South Wales Electricity Board: miscellaneous records, 1961-1997 (D/D El/S)

Fish merchants

W R Jones, Wholesale Fish Merchant, Swansea: fishing records and photographs of Swansea South Dock, 1912-1957 (D/D X 13)

Flour mills

Weaver and Company: plan of Swansea flour mill, 1940s (D142)

Gas undertakings

Ammanford Gas Undertaking: account books, 1951-1966 (D/D Ga/Am)

Gowerton Gas Undertaking: account books and share records, 1908-1960 (D/D Ga/G)

Llanelli Gas Undertaking: cash book, 1967-1971 (D/D Ga/Lly)

Neath Gas Undertaking: records, 1866-1971, including a large number of engineering drawings (D/D Ga/N)

Pontardawe Gas Undertaking: records, 1908-1966 (D/D Ga/Pd)

Pontarddulais Gas Undertaking: records, 1877-1962 (D/D Ga/P)

Port Talbot Gas Undertaking: records, 1890-1972, including engineering drawings (D/D Ga/PT)

Swansea Gas Undertaking (Swansea Gaslight Company): records, including Acts of Parliament, minutes, correspondence, plans and photographs, 1826-1971 (D/D Ga/S)

Iron and steel makers and founders

Amman Iron Company: business records, 1859-1920 (D/D SB 13)

Briton Ferry Iron Works: miscellaneous items, 1890-1900 (D/D Xlm)

Briton Ferry Steel Company Ltd: directors' reports and brochure, 1938 (D/D Z 20)

Crane Foundry, Ystradgynlais: records, 1898-1922 (D/D Yc)

Cross Foundry, Gorseinon: records, 1881-1908 (D/D CV 4)

Express Steel Company, Cwmavon: memorandum and articles of association, 1897 (D/D Xlm)

Gilbertson of Pontardawe, steelmakers: letter books, 1890-1929; other correspondence, 1883-1932, and plans (D/D Gil); accounts, 1861-1929 (D/D X 259)

Grovesend Steel and Tinplate Company: records, 1909-1930 (D/D CV 4)

Bernard Hastie and Company Ltd: history, 1987 (D/D Z 246)

P Jenkins' Sons Ltd, metalfounders, Excelsior Works, Neath: records, 1893-1928, mostly business correspondence (D/D PJ)

Neath Abbey Ironworks Company: Neath Abbey Iron Works was built by the Quaker firm of Fox and Company of Cornwall in 1792. Its products, which included stationary and marine engines and locomotives, were sent principally across South Wales, but also worldwide. The works closed in 1875, then, after an attempted revival, finally in 1885. Over 7,500 extant drawings show the development of engines and industrial machinery, 1792-1892, the majority of plans being from the middle of the century. (D/D NAI, *restricted access:* only by prior written permission from the County Archivist)

Plans of gas installations and work for gas contracts, 1820-1874 (D/D NAI/G)

Locomotive and railway engineering plans, 1826-1892 (D/D NAI/L)

Plans of machinery, 1792-1882 (D/D NAI/M)

Ship and marine engineering plans, 1817-1883 (D/D NAI/S)

Plans of the Neath Abbey Iron Works, 1813-1881, including ground plans, plans of buildings, inventories of stock, plans of engines and machinery for the furnaces, boring mill, fitting shop, rolling mill, wharf, Cheadle Works and Neath Abbey Gas Works (D/D NAI/W)

Port Talbot and Margam Steelworks: miscellaneous records, 1918-1964; plan, *circa* 1935 (D/D Xlm); programme for opening of new strip mill, 1986 (D/D X 46); publicity material for BSC Port Talbot Division, including cine film, 1940s-1980s (D/D Z 208)

Richard Thomas and Baldwin Company: plans of steel and tinplate works in West Glamorgan, *circa* 1930-1950 (D/D Z 75)

Richard Thomas and Company Ltd: microfilm (unsorted and undated) (D103)

Swansea Foundry: various records (unsorted and undated) (D190)

Swansea Steel Company Ltd: insurance certificates, 1901-1905 (D103)

Ynyscedwyn Furnaces: records, 1801-1875 (D/D Yc)

Miscellaneous: cine films on the Steel Company of Wales development projects, 1948-1950 (D/D Z 278); map of South Wales showing all old-type steel mills, produced by the British Steel Corporation, 1978 (D/D Z 150)

Metal trading

Letter home from the wife of a Swansea copper trader based in Coquimbo, Chile, 1905 (D/D Z 203)

Annual reports of the Swansea Royal Metal Exchange, 1924-1935 (D/D Z 21)

Nickel smelting

Photograph of the Mond Nickel Works, Clydach, after 1948 (D140); history of the Mond Nickel Company Ltd, 1918 (D247)

Oil refineries

Brochure for Llandarcy oil refinery, n.d. [1920s] (D/D Z 212)

Public houses

Sale catalogue of public houses in Swansea and Llangiwg, 1919 (D/D Xcx)

Plans of public houses in Swansea and South Wales, *circa* 1920-1940 (D/D Z 158)

Railway companies

Briton Ferry Docks Company: register of probate, 1855-1867 (D/D PRO/BRB)

Dulais Valley Mineral Railway Company: proprietors' ledger, share register and register of share transfers, 1862-1892 (D/D PRO/BRB)

Gower Light Railway: draft order, 1896 (D/D Xau); plans for the intended line of the railway, 1896 (D/D P)

Great Western Railway Company/British Railways Board: miscellaneous records, including train registers for King's Dock signal box, 1922-1985 (D108)

Neath and Brecon Railway Company: share registers, registers of share transfers and of probate, 1870-1922 (D/D PRO/BRB); contract, 1865 (D/D Z 1)

Port Talbot Railway and Dock Company: share registers, share conversion registers, registers of share transfers and of probate, 1895-1922 (D/D PRO/BRB); staff register, 1908-1911; dredging reports, 1899-1901 (D/D Xnd); photograph album, *circa* 1900 (D/D Z 276)

Rhondda and Swansea Bay Railway Company: share registers, share conversion registers, registers of share transfers and of probate, 1890-1922 (D/D PRO/BRB); Rhondda and Swansea Bay Railway Acts, 1882-1898 (NL and D/D Z 25); papers relating to the Company, 1890-1908, including plans (D/D BF); miscellaneous records, 1880-1897 (SL)

South Wales Mineral Railway Company: share registers, 1900-1921 (D/D PRO/BRB); South Wales Mineral Railway Act, 1853 (D/D X 8)

South Wales Railway: specification for the Swansea to Llanelli section, *circa* 1855 (D/D Z 62)

Swansea and Mumbles Railway: legal records and associated correspondence, 1804-1953 (D/D SB 9); photographs and printed material, *circa* 1890-1994 (D/D Z 303); various papers concerned with the 175th anniversary of the Mumbles Railway, 1970s (D194); feasibility study into reopening, 1989 (D/D Z 101)

Vale of Neath Railway: share conversion register and register of probate, 1847-1870 (includes address on the opening of the Vale of Neath Railway, 1863) (D/D PRO/BRB)

Copies of local railway bills and associated correspondence: Brynaman and Neath Railway Bill, 1902; Briton Ferry Docks and Railway Act, 1851; Great Western Railway Bills, 1889, 1904 and 1911; Great Western Railway Neath River Crossing Bill, 1892; Neath, Pontardawe and Brynaman Railway Bills, 1895 and 1904; Rhondda and Swansea Bay Railway Bills, 1882, 1883, 1885, 1891, 1893 and 1895; South Wales Mineral Railway Bill, 1907; opposition to the Railway and Canal Traffic Act, 1888; miscellaneous other Local Railway Acts, 1845-1931; Neath Corporation Tramways Bill, 1897 (NL)

Scrap metal merchants

E Morton Peel Ltd, scrap metal merchants, Swansea: records, 1937-1965 (D210)

Shops and department stores

D L Davies and Son, men's outfitters, Swansea: records, 1931-1969 (D138)

Goldstone and Company, antique dealers, Swansea: account books, 1926-1933 (D/D Z 20)

John Lewis and Company, general merchants, Briton Ferry: account book, 1915-1922 (D/D Z 19)

Lewis Lewis (Swansea) Ltd: records, 1870-1974 (D71 and D85)

Morris Family Butchers of Gowerton: accounts, 1887-1935, and poster, 1896 (D/D Z 188)

Pandy Stores, Pontrhydyfen: ledgers, 1929-1946 (D/D X 241)

T Williams, grocer, Port Talbot: accounts, 1947-1980 (D/D Z 24)

Stained glass studios

Celtic Stained Glass Studios, Swansea: papers relating to the design and installation of stained glass in Britain and abroad, 1948-1992 (partly listed) (D/D Cel)

Sulphuric acid manufacturers

F W Berke and Company Ltd, dealers in sulphuric acid, Morriston: cash book, 1919-1939 (D224)

Timber merchants

Gregor Bros of Swansea: annual reports and accounts, 1953-1975 (D/D Z 283)

Tinplate works

Aber Tinplate Works: share records, 1902-1916 (D103)

Cilfrew Tinplate Works: plan, 1907 (D/D Z 75)

Clayton Tinplate Works, Pontarddulais: correspondence and accounts, 1937-1972 (D/D Z 68)

Copper Miners Tinplate Company, Cwmavon: memorandum of association and plan of works, 1897 (D/D Xlm); addresses to Governors and Directors, 1852-1867 (D/D X 93)

Cwmfelin Steel and Tinplate Company: share records, 1890-1918 (D103); tinplate card commemorating visit of Prince of Wales to the Cwmfelin Works, 1919 (D151)

Elba Tinplate Works, Gowerton: photographs, n.d. (D/D Z 75)

Glanrhyd Tinplate Company: accounts, 1919-1934 (D/D X 259)

Grovesend Steel and Tinplate Company: records, 1909-1930 (D/D CV 4); salaries accounts, 1918-1939 (D/D Z 69)

Gurnos Brick and Tinplate Works: records, 1877-1920 (D/D Yc)

Melyn Tinplate Works: minutes, 1865-1920 (D/D Xgu); deeds, 1865-1892 (D/D Xhw)

Richard Thomas and Baldwin Company: plans of steel and tinplate works in West Glamorgan, *circa* 1930-1950 (D/D Z 75)

Upper Forest Tinplate Works, Morriston: lease, 1890 (D/D Z 75)

Ynyscedwyn Tinplate Works: records, 1891-1925 (D/D Yc)

Ynyspenllwch Tinplate Works: accounts, 1868-1870 (D/D X 323)

Tramway companies

Neath Tramways: video on the history of the Neath gas tram, 1995 (D/D Z 255)

Swansea Improvement and Tramways Company: deeds, 1807-1888 (D/D Xge)

See also *Swansea and Mumbles Railway* in the section above, *Railway companies.*

Undertakers

Ivor Griffiths and Company, undertakers, Morriston: papers, 1908-1978 (D182)

Woollen manufacturers

William J Jones, woollen manufacturer, Pontarddulais: accounts, 1896-1926 (D/D Z 159)

Zinc works

John Corfield, spelter manufacturers, Swansea: biographical notes on John Corfield (1859-1917) of Swansea, 1997 (D/D Z 300)

Tonnage book for goods carried on the Neath and Swansea Red Jacket and Junction Canals, afterwards the Tennant Canal, 1824 (D/D T 1041)

MARITIME RECORDS

Swansea Harbour

Plans of proposed improvements to the harbour (mostly copies), 1771-1852 (D/D WCR/Pl)

Swansea Harbour Act, 1791 (D/D Z 190)

Volume of reports, correspondence and plans relating to the harbour, 1794-1847 (D/D Z 207)

Swansea Harbour Act, 1836 (D/D Z 307)

Contract drawings for docks and quayside structures, 1836-1937 (D/D SHa)

Reports on the openings of Swansea's docks, 1850-1881 (D/D Xgb)

Swansea Harbour Acts, 1861 and 1894 (D/D Z 299)

Article on outbreak of yellow fever in the Port of Swansea in 1865 (D/D Z 189)

Share prospectus, 1878 (D/D Xty)

Ephemera relating to the opening of the Prince of Wales Dock, 1881 (SL WM)

Swansea Port Health Authority: annual reports, 1895-date; financial records, 1885-1958 (PH); reports of the Medical Officer of Health, 1934-1939 (TC 71)

Swansea Port Sanitary Authority: minutes, 1888-1972 (TC 71)

Records of Felix Martin & Company, ship's chandlers and instrument repairers, 1897-1962 (D26)

Shipping records of Charles Huss and Company Ltd, 1902-1917 (D45)

Swansea Harbour Trust: warrant book, 1908-1910 (D195)

W R Jones, Wholesale Fish Merchant, Swansea: fishing records and photographs of Swansea South Dock, 1912-1957 (D/D X 13)

Tables showing Swansea Harbour trade, 1914 (D/D Z 21)

Coastlines Ltd: cargo manifests, 1920-1930 (D135)

Swansea Harbour Trust: share registers and share conversion registers, 1921-1923 (D/D PRO/BRB)

Port of Swansea: coal-lading manifests, 1920s-1970s (D120)

Registers of protests of ship's masters before public notary, 1936-1979 (D/D SB 2)

Prince of Wales Dry Dock Company: miscellanea, *circa* 1950-1980 (D/D Z 80)

Plans of the Swansea pilot cutter, *Seamark*, 1958 (D232)

History of the Royal Naval Reserve Swansea Unit, 1993 (D/D Z 162)

Great Western Railway and Docks Board papers (unsorted and unlisted) (D2)

Shipping records of Poingdestre & Mesnier & Cie (unsorted and unlisted) (D3)

Shipping records of Stone and Rolfe Ltd and Thomas Stone & Co Ltd, (unsorted and unlisted) (D130 and D131)

British Transport Commission Shipping lists (unsorted and unlisted) (D154)

Docks and Inland Waterway Executive shipping lists (unsorted and unlisted) (D155)

Neath Harbour

Minutes, 1871-1928; correspondence, 1864-1937; accounts, 1862-1937 (includes ledgers giving names of vessels and analyses of cargoes, 1862-1928); registers of arrivals and sailings, 1915-1948; plans, 1842-1944 (D/D NHa, *restricted access:* only by prior written permission from the County Archivist)

Share prospectus, 1882 (D/D Xty)

Port Talbot Harbour

Aberavon Harbour Act, 1836 (D/D Xkh)

Port Talbot Pilotage Authority: registers of pilotage and vessels entering and leaving the port, 1895-1951; pilotage returns, 1913-1933; logbooks of pilot cutter *Marian Byass*, 1934-1952; bye-laws, 1924; correspondence, 1904-1923; accounts, 1936-1955 (PTL PTHa)

Miscellaneous harbour records, *circa* 1890-1920 (unsorted and unlisted) (D/D PTHa)

Reports on entrance and channel works at Port Talbot Harbour, 1899-1901 (D/D Xnd)

Record books of arrivals and sailings, 1899-1968 (D/D Xlm)

Harbour dues book, 1900-1936 (D/D Z 148)

Port Talbot Pilotage Cutter Company: minutes, 1912-1934; register of towages, 1931-1934; accounts, 1912-1945 (PTL PTHa)

Sea charts

Sea chart of Swansea Bay, 1830 (modern reprint) (D/D Z 172)

Egbert Moxham's sea chart of Swansea Bay, 1846 (D/D Z 179)

Sea chart, St Govan's Head to Mumbles, 1888 (D/D P)

Sea chart, South Pembrokeshire to Cardiff, 1952 (D/D Z 137)

Other records

Record of shipwrecks on the Glamorgan coast, 1778-1780 (D/D Gn)

List of vessels saved and lost at Newton and neighbourhood, 1797-1818 (D/D Xhf)

Log book of the *Culloden xxxdoris* [last word illegible], 1806-1808 (D/D Ma)

Log book of the barque *Fidelity*, 1847-1848 (PTL)

Sailor's letter recounting a voyage from Swansea to Valparaiso, 1848 (D/D Z 195)

Royal National Lifeboat Institution (Mumbles Lifeboat): minutes, 1863-1980; returns of service (record of lifeboat incidents), 1931-1981; lifeboat inspector's visiting books, 1939-1983; financial records, 1945-1958; plans, 1924-1951 (D/D RNLI/M)

Transcript of the log of the barque *Cornwall* on voyage to South America, 1867-1868 (D/D Z 164)

Letter from sailor on copper barque *Uncas* on voyage to Chile, *circa* 1870 (D14)

Correspondence concerning coastguard houses at Rhossili, 1890-1892 (D/D P)

Diary of the master of the SS *Ladstock* voyaging to Chile (in Welsh), 1900-1901 (D/D Z 77)

Photograph of the Port Eynon lifeboat, before 1916 (D/D Xug)

Documents concerning HMS *Arethusa*, 1934-1944 (D89)

Map showing approximate sites of shipwrecks around the Gower peninsula, 1985 (D/D Z 43)

For other maritime records, see also the sections above *Registry of Shipping* and *South Wales Sea Fisheries Committee*.

RECORDS OF SOCIETIES, SPORT AND THE ARTS

Aberavon and Port Talbot District Nursing Association: minutes, 1898-1959; miscellaneous records, 1899-1973 (PTL PTNA)

Aberavon Townswomen's Guild: records, 1959-1986 (D/D ATG)

Amicable Society of Llansamlet: accounts, 1796-1861 (D/D Z 44)

Ancient Order of Foresters, Swansea Branch: contributions book, 1934-1963 (D/D Z 193)

Association of Bookmen of Swansea and West Wales: constitution, *circa* 1943; minutes, 1943-1961; accounts, 1946-1964; correspondence, 1948-1962 (SL AB)

Baglan Rifle Range Association: correspondence and plans, 1909-1914 (PTL)

British Association for the Advancement of Science: programme of excursions, Swansea, 1880 (D252)

British Medical Association, South Wales and Monmouthshire Branch: minutes, 1903-1979 (D/D BMA/S); Swansea Division Emergency Committee: minutes, 1939-1948 (D238)

Briton Ferry Debating Society: minutes, 1906-1962 (NL)

Caradog ap Iestyn Lodge of True Ivorites: minutes, 1864-1935 (PTL); correspondence, 1913-1916 (D/D Bap)

Eisteddfodau: List of competitors and winners, 1932 (PTL); file on the Lliw Valley Eisteddfod of 1980, 1975-1978 (D/D X 46); programmes, 1976-1996 (D/D Z 224)

Electrical Association of Women, Swansea Branch: records, 1954-1981 (D52)

Ffynone Club, Swansea: records, 1876-1990 (D164)

First Mumbles Scout Group: papers, 1914-1985 (D250)

Girl Guide Association, West Glamorgan Branch: charter and bye-laws, 1949; minutes, 1922-1993; annual reports, 1917-1995 (with gaps); publications, 1937-1981; programmes and other memorabilia, 1960s-1990s; correspondence, 1916-1989 (D/D Gui/W)

Gower Festival: records, 1977-1981 (D62)

Gower Ornithological Society: minutes, 1956-1985; rules, 1956-1981; correspondence, 1957-1986; periodicals, 1956-1985 (D/D GOS)

Gower Society: records, 1947-date (D56); papers of Dr Gwent Jones concerning the Gower Society, 1948-1968 (D157)

Gowerton Rifle Range Association: correspondence and plans, 1913-1918 (PTL)

Gwaun-Cae-Gurwen Miners' Welfare Hall Management Committee: minutes, 1941-1962 (D/D GWH)

Historical Association, Swansea Branch: records, 1928-1982 (D72)

Independent Order of Oddfellows, Loyal James Jones Lodge, Swansea Branch: accounts, 1909-1924 (D/D Z 327)

Independent Order of Rechabites, Clydach Tent: minutes, annual reports, sickness payment registers, accounts and correspondence, 1883-1933 (D/D CR)

Jersey Marine Golf Club: photograph of opening, 1902 (D/D Z 10)

Loyal Cambrian Independent Order of Loyal Alfreds: annual statements, 1892-1899 (D171)

Maesteg Drill Hall Association: correspondence and plans, 1912-1913 (PTL)

Margam Cricket Club: scoring books, 1925-1933 (D/D Z 24); fixtures list, 1968, (D/D Z 25)

Morriston Annual Eisteddfod: programmes, 1907-1933 (D139)

Morriston Orpheus Choir: newscuttings and programmes, 1960-1968 (D69)

Mothers' Union, Diocese of Swansea and Brecon: history, 1989 (D/D MU/S)

Mumbles and District Conservation Society: minutes and photographs, 1971-1978 (D21)

Mumbles Townswomen's Guild: scrapbook, 1969-1983 (D/D MTG)

Neath Billiard Club: accounts, 1914-1924 (D/D Z 157)

Old Glanmorians Association: records, 1929-date (D213); press cuttings etc, various dates (D233)

Parc Beck Allotment Society: minutes, 1963-1989; letter books, 1979-1993; registers of members, 1962-1988; financial and legal records, 1920-1989 (D/D PBAS)

Pontardawe Public Hall and Institute: minutes, 1907-1974; account books, 1909-1982 (D/D PPH)

Pontarddulais Townswomen's Guild: minutes and accounts, 1957-1959 (D/D Z 268)

Port Talbot Little Theatre: programmes, 1969-1991 (D/D Z 25)

Port Talbot Municipal Choir: minutes and accounts, 1950-1980 (D/D Z 24)

Port Talbot Tennis Club: minutes, 1910-1955 (D/D Xlm)

Royal Antediluvian Order of Buffaloes, Jersey Lodge: minutes, 1918-1921; membership register, 1915-1924 (D/D X 9)

Royal Institution of South Wales: annual reports, 1838-1912 (with gaps); poster, 1842 (D/D RISW)

Royal National Lifeboat Institution (Mumbles Lifeboat): minutes, 1863-1980; returns of service (record of lifeboat incidents), 1931-1981; lifeboat inspector's visiting books, 1939-1983; financial records, 1945-1958; plans, 1924-1951 (D/D RNLI/M)

St John Ambulance Association, Swansea Branch: records, 1901-1927 (D133)

Sketty Ambulance Depot Social Committee: minute book, 1940-1945 (D167)

Sketty Church Men's Club and Institute: records, 1911-1989 (D172)

Soroptimists International, Port Talbot Branch: minutes, 1963-1980; accounts, 1948-1987 (D/D Z 49)

South Wales Mountaineering Club: minutes, 1980-1993; newsletters, 1980-1994 (D/D SWMC)

Swansea Boy Scouts: papers on scouting in Swansea, 1907-1976 (D8)

Swansea City Football Club: see under *Swansea Town Football Club*

Swansea and District Federation of the Church of England Men's Society: constitution, 1922; minutes, 1910-1924; accounts, 1915-1923; correspondence, 1914-1923 (SL CE)

Swansea and District Male Voice Choir: miscellaneous documents, 1924-1939 (D63)

Swansea Dragons American Football Club: match programme, n.d. (D112)

Swansea Festival: records, 1948-date (D59)

Swansea Grand Theatre: assorted photographs, n.d. (D96); programmes, 1935-57 (D47 and D50); programmes and newscuttings, 1958-1964 (D206). See also sections above *Boroughs* and *District Councils 1974-1996*

Swansea Hospital Linen Guild: minutes, 1940-1948 (D188)

Swansea Housing Group: newsletters, 1995-1997; annual report, 1996 (D/D SHG)

Swansea Little Theatre: records, 1924-date (D102, *restricted access:* only by prior written permission from the County Archivist); documents relating to the Little Theatre, n.d. (D215)

Swansea Municipal Choir: scrapbook recording activities of the choir, 1944-1957 (D265)

Swansea Round Table: history, 1983 (D/D Z 4)

Swansea and South Wales Institution for the Blind: souvenir booklet, 1935 (D/D SIB)

Swansea and South West Wales District Society of Incorporated Accountants: minutes, 1932-1948 (SL)

Swansea Theatre Tontine: minutes, 1855-1891; accounts, 1805-1891; list of subscribers, 1805; rules, 1875; legal papers, 1857-1882; correspondence, 1826-1889; history, 1878 (SL WM)

Swansea Town/City Football Club: papers relating to the Club, 1921-date (D219); match programmes, n.d. (unlisted) (D84); Swansea Town AFC Supporters Club: minutes, 1954-1966 (D80)

Swansea Valley Historical Society: records, photographs and publications relating to the upper Swansea Valley, 1800-1981 (D/D HSV)

Swansea Working Men's Club: minutes, 1922-1982; deeds and related documents, n.d.; journals, n.d. (unsorted and unlisted)

United Nations Association, Swansea Branch: papers, 1947-1993 (D251)

Welsh Sculpture Trust: memorandum of association, 1981 (D/D Z 5)

Women's Gas Federation, Swansea Branch: constitution, *circa* 1950s; minutes, 1974-1987; press cuttings and photographs, 1959-1994 (D/D WGF); **Port Talbot Branch:** records, 1964-1987 (D/D Xlm)

Women's Institute, Bryncoch Branch: survey of St Matthew's Church, Dyffryn (D/D Xno 31) **Pendoylan Branch:** minutes, 1965-1981; record books, 1965-1987 (D/D Xno 17); **Penmaen and Nicholaston Branch:** minute books, 1922-1972; monthly record books, 1926-1978; annual reports, 1935-1980; scrapbook, 1965 (D/D Xno 15); **Rhossili Branch:** minutes, 1933-1952 (D/D Xno 26); **various Gower branches**: scrapbooks compiled for jubilee of WI, 1965 (D/D Xno 18-25)

Personal papers of individuals connected with the arts

Papers of **W Grant Murray**, Director of Art for the County Borough of Swansea, 1910-1934 (D201)

Letters of **Adelina Patti** to Mrs Ada Lloyd, 1903-1906 and 1914-1918, also photographs, *circa* 1905 (D/D X 237); letter to Mr Vivian, 1893 (D/D Z 45)

Letter from **Dylan Thomas**, 1951 (D/D Z 309); recordings of broadcasts by Dylan Thomas, n.d. (D/D Z 266 and 309)

Papers of **Edgar Williams**, cellist, 1926-1956 (D173)

Miscellaneous music programmes for events in Swansea, 1905-1976 (D220)

Members Names 1799	January 1 1799	February 5	March 2nd	April 5	May 7th	June 14	July 2nd	August 6th	September 3rd	October 1st	November	December 3
1	Rees David Copper	3		3	1	·		3			3	
2	Morgan Owen Copper	3	1	·	·	3	·		3	·	2	·
3	David William		2	·	3	·	2	·	·	3	·	
4	Peter King	·		3	1	1	·		3	·	3	·
5	Morgan Wallis			3	·	·	3			3	·	3
6	Robert Jones	2	1	1	1	·	2	1	·	2	·	3
7	John Howell	·		3	·	3	·		3	·	3	
8	Morgan Lewis	·		3	·	3		Deceas				
9	Morg. David Sinker	3	·	·	3	1	·	2	·	·	3	· 2
10	Hopkin Morgan Farmer	1	1	1	1	1	·	2	1	·	2	1
11	Henry David Copper	·		3	1	1	1	1	1	1	1	
12	William John Farmer	2	·		3	·	2	·	2	·	2	· 2
13	David Morgan Smith	1		2	·	2	·	2	·	2	1	2
14	Richard Ferguin	·	2	·		3	·		3	·	2	·
15	George Evans	·	3	·	3	·	·		3	1	1	1
16	Morgan John	·	3	·	·	3	·	2	1	1	1	·
17	Rees Roby Ostler	1	1	1	1	1	1	1	·	2	·	2
18	Thos. Richards Serv.	·		3	·	·	3	·	·	3	·	3
19	Philip Thomas Copp	·	3	·	·	3	·	·	3	·	3	·
20	Thos. William Sinker	3	·	·	3	·	·	3	·	3	·	2
21	John David Ostler	·	·	3	·	·	3	·	·	3	·	3
22	Joshua David Sinker	·	3	·	·	3	·	·	3	·	3	·
23		·	2	·	·	3	·	Decea			

Entries from the account book of the Amicable Society of Llansamlet for 1799 (D/D Z 44/1)

RECORDS OF POLITICAL PARTIES, CO-OPERATIVE SOCIETIES AND TRADES UNIONS

Labour Party

Gwaun-Cae-Gurwen Labour Party: minutes, 1963-1990 (D/D Z 183)

Lliw Valley District Labour Party: minutes, agendas, correspondence and financial records, 1987-1996 (Lab/Lli, *restricted access:* only by prior written permission from the County Archivist)

Neath Borough Council Labour Group: minutes, 1965-1974 (Lab/N)

Penderry Labour Women's Section: minutes, 1935-1985; accounts, 1969-1985 (D185)

Swansea Labour Association: records, 1902-1971 (D77, *restricted access:* only by prior written permission from the County Archivist)

Swansea Labour Group: minutes, 1932-1942, 1957-1974 (D78, *restricted access:* only by prior written permission from the County Archivist)

Trades Unions

Amalgamated Society of Woodworkers, Swansea Branch: minutes, 1921-1924 (D/D Z 106)

British Steel Smelters Amalgamated Association: monthly reports, 1899-1902 (D/D Z 42)

National Federation of Sub Postmasters, Swansea Branch: minutes, 1921-1944 (D/D X 48)

National Union of Mineworkers, Avon Colliery Lodge: minutes, 1948-1970; minutes of area delegate conferences, 1954-1956 (D/D X 8)

National Union of Miners, Seven Sisters Lodge: records, 1911-1964 (D/D Xkx)

National Union of Mineworkers, Tarreni Lodge: minutes and correspondence, 1936-1949 (D/D X 125)

South Wales and Monmouthshire Colliery Examiners' Association, Mardy Lodge: minutes and accounts, 1920-1949 (D/D Z 144)

South Wales and Monmouthshire Winding Enginemen's Association, Swansea Branch: minutes, 1944-1948 (D/D Z 3)

Swansea Trades Union Unemployed Association: minutes and correspondence, 1932-1939 (D79)

Co-operative Societies

Alltwen and Pontardawe Co-operative Society: records, 1888-1981
(D/D Co-op All)

Briton Ferry and Neath Co-operative Society: minutes, 1916-1975
(D/D Co-op BFN)

Craig Cefn Parc Co-operative Society: accounts, 1889 (D/D Z 330)

Cwmgorse Co-operative Society: minutes, 1957-1961 (D/D Co-op All)

Swansea Co-operative Society: minutes, 1954-1971 (D/D Co-op S)

Personal papers of individuals involved in politics

Papers of **John Graham Ball**, Plaid Cymru Councillor (Swansea), 1973-1979 (D116)

Papers of Alderman **William Jones Davies** (Swansea), 1914-1945 (D128)

Papers of **D R Grenfell**, MP for Gower, 1917-1960 (D207)

Papers of Cllr **T S Harris** (Swansea), 1917-1966 (D180)

Items relating to Cllr **Richard Henry** JP, Mayor of Swansea, 1936-1937 (D192)

Papers of Cllr **W T Mainwaring Hughes**, Independent (Swansea), 1930-1976 (D23)

Newscuttings and correspondence of **Geoffrey Clegg Hutchinson** relating to his candidacy for the Gower constituency in the general election of 1935 (D16)

Items relating to **Sam Knight**, founder member of the Communist Party of Great Britain, 1970s-1980s (D99)

Papers of Alderman **David Matthews**, Liberal (Swansea), 1918-1959 (D97)

Papers of Alderman **Percy Morris** (Swansea), 1935-1972 (D53)

Papers of **David Williams** (1865-1941), Labour MP for Swansea East, 1922-1940 (D266)

Biography of Reverend **John Williams** MP, n.d. (D176)

OTHER SOURCES

MAPS AND PLANS

Estate maps

Estate collections contain many fine examples of manuscript maps: these are listed above in the section *Estate and Family Records* under the name of the estate. A detailed list may be found in the publication *A Catalogue of Glamorgan Estate Maps*, by Hilary M Thomas (Glamorgan Archives, 1992).

Tithe maps

The Archive Service holds original or photocopy awards (map and accompanying apportionment) *circa* 1840 for all parishes in West Glamorgan except for Briton Ferry and Margam, for which no awards were made. Following the Tithe Commutation Act 1836, which appointed Commissioners to deal with the commutation of tithes from payments in kind to payment in money, every parish in England and Wales was surveyed and a map drawn with an accompanying apportionment in the form of a schedule which listed landowner, tenant, property, acreage and tithe payable. These plans are the earliest large-scale maps to have been made of complete parishes.

Ordnance Survey maps

There is an extensive range of Ordnance Survey maps dating from the 1870s to the 1970s. The most commonly used scale for local history research is 1:2500, approximately 25" to the mile, and county editions for Glamorgan were published around the years 1876 (1st edition), 1897 (2nd edition), 1916 (3rd edition) and 1922-1940 (revised 3rd edition). Coverage for the first and third editions is almost complete for Glamorgan.

There are some sea charts and plans of harbour facilities listed in the section *Maritime Records*. Colliery plans are also listed above in the section *Other Public Records*. Listed below are maps in miscellaneous collections which are not grouped elsewhere in this guide.

Maps of South Wales and Glamorgan

John Speed's map of Glamorgan, 1610 (D/D Z 134)
Christopher Saxton's map of Glamorgan, *circa* 1610 (D/D Z 134)
John Ogilby's ribbon road map, Monmouth to Briton Ferry, 1675 (D/D Z 134)
Robert Morden's map of Glamorgan, *circa* 1701 (D/D Z 134)
Emmanuel Bowen's road map from Llandaff to Llanstephan, 1720 (D/D Xlm)
Thomas Kitchin's map of Glamorgan, *circa* 1750 (D/D Z 134)
John Williams' road map from Gorseinon to Neath, 1779 (D/D Xdp)
Road map from the New Passage to Llanelli, 1798 (D/D Xlm)
George Yates' map of Glamorgan, 1799 (D/D Z 134)

Map of proposed mail road from Carmarthen to Pyle, with detail of Briton Ferry, by Thomas Telford, 1824 (D/D Xx)

Road and railway map of Glamorgan by Gall and Inglis, before 1880 (D/D Z 72)

Bacon's map of South Wales, *circa* 1900, (D/D X 34)

Plans of the South Wales Coalfield, 1908-1915 (D/D Xgb)

Map of the Great Western Railway network, 1930s (D/D Z 129)

German target maps of South Wales, 1941 (D263 and D/D Z 290)

Map of South Wales showing all old-type steel mills, produced by the British Steel Corporation, 1978 (D/D Z 150)

Maps of Swansea

Plan of Swansea Town, 1851 (SL)

Boundaries of the Borough of Swansea, 1867 (D/D Xdp)

Goad insurance plans of the centre of Swansea, 1929 (D/D Xgb), 1888-1961 (D/D Z 319) and 1938 (unlisted)

Wyld's plan of Swansea, late 19th century (SL)

Street plan of Swansea, 1930s (D/D Xgb)

Maps of Neath

Plan of Neath, 1720 (D/D Z 87)

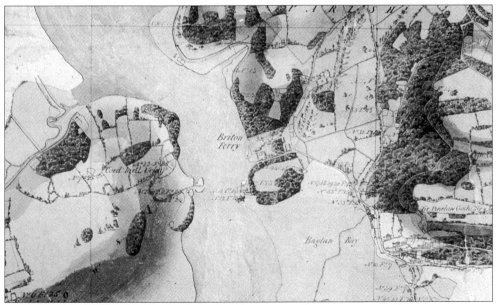

Detail from a map of the Briton Ferry Estate by Thomas Hornor showing Briton Ferry, 1815 (D/D BF/E 157A)

PICTURES AND PHOTOGRAPHS

As mentioned above in the section *Antiquarian Collections*, the late Rowland Morton Davies created the nucleus of a civic picture collection maintained by the former Swansea City Council. This collection, which is arranged in boxes by subject, covers the whole of the City of Swansea in its pre-1996 boundaries, as well as a few boxes of pictures from beyond Swansea. The arrangement of the boxes is as follows:

Aerial views; Mumbles Train; Lower Town; the Strand; Wind Street; Swansea Castle; Castle Square and Castle Bailey Street; Castle Street; Castle Gardens; Temple Street; Princess Way; Oxford Street; Swansea Markets; places of entertainment; Cradock Street to Portland Street; St Mary's Church and Square; the Quadrant area; College Street; Orchard Street; Bellevue Way to Clifton Hill; Kingsway; High Street; Alexandra Road; Mount Pleasant; Mansel Street to De la Beche Street; Walter Road; St Helen's Road; Sandfields; Brynymor Road to St Helen's Avenue; Victoria Park; the Guildhall; St Helen's; Brynmill; Uplands; the University and Singleton Hospital; Singleton Park; Brynmill Park; Cwmdonkin Park; Glanmor and Cwmgwyn; Sketty; Tycoch and Hendrefoilan; Killay and Wimmerfield; Dunvant; Townhill and Mayhill; Cockett; Waunarlwydd; Fforestfach to Penlan, Portmead and Blaen-y-maes; Cwmbwrla; Manselton; Brynhyfryd; Treboeth; Dyfatty to Hafod; Landore and Plasmarl; Morriston; M4 Morriston by-pass; Llansamlet; Birchgrove; Swansea Valley to Clydach; Pontardawe and upper Swansea Valley; St Thomas; Port Tennant and Danygraig; Kilvey and Crymlyn; Bonymaen and east side Swansea Valley; Derwen Fawr; Ashleigh Road; Blackpill; Clyne; Mayals; West Cross and Norton; Mumbles Road; Oystermouth to Caswell; Gower; Lliw Valley; Carmarthenshire; Neath and Port Talbot; Swansea personages; transport; trams; Port of Swansea; canals and trains; River Tawe; Swansea foreshore; the Blitz; maps and plans; Swansea Leisure Centre; lower Swansea Valley; 1969 royal visit and city status; Dylan Thomas; Maritime Quarter; 1973 royal visit; Swansea mayors; council estates; schools; civic ceremonies (P/PR and P/SL)

Photographs are also to be found in miscellaneous collections, either separately or with other records. Photographs of people can sometimes be found amongst estate and family papers, and these are listed in the section above, *Estate and Family Records*. The photographs listed below are those which cannot be grouped elsewhere in this guide. They are arranged in date order, although their subject matter is diverse.

Microfiche copies of the Francis Frith Archive, 1860-1970, showing views from all over West Glamorgan (D/D Xgb)
White Rock Ferry, n.d. [mid 19th century], (D/D Z 21)
Cwmavon and district, views, *circa* 1890-1900 (D/D Xlp)
Victorian/Edwardian views of Swansea (D137)
Photographs of Swansea and Gower, 19th and 20th centuries (D/D Z 207)

Postcards of West Glamorgan, 19th and 20th centuries (unlisted) (D/D DH)

Photograph collection of Arthur Hill, mostly of Swansea and Gower, *circa* 1880s-1970s (D/D AWH)

Photograph albums of William Oldham of Swansea, mostly of Swansea and Gower, *circa* 1900-1910 (D/D Z 219)

Postcards of Swansea and Gower, *circa* 1900-1950 (D/D Z 303)

Photograph album of views in West Glamorgan, particularly Port Talbot and Margam, *circa* 1900-1985 (D/D Z 250)

Photograph and postcard album of Marie Hullin of Mumbles, *circa* 1910-1960 (D/D Z 230)

Photograph albums of the Swansea Rifles and the Welch Regiment, First World War (D147)

40 lantern slides of First World War scenes, Northern France (D30)

Photographs of Gower and Swansea, 1930s (D/D Z 132)

Auxiliary Fire Service photograph album, 1939-1941 (D235)

Swansea after the Blitz, 1941 (D227)

British troops in Belgium, 1944-1945 (D/D Z 8)

Photograph album including pictures of Swansea after the Blitz, [1940s] (D184)

Publicity photographs of West Glamorgan, 1950s-1960s (D/D Z 201)

Photographs of the Briton Ferry area, 1989-1990 (D/D Z 250)

Photograph albums, postcards and photographs of Swansea, various dates (D36, D39, D209 and D267)

Slide collection of J M Davies, n.d. (D226)

Photograph album of journey through South Wales, n.d. (D259)

Miscellaneous photographs relating to South Wales regiments, n.d. (D165)

Miscellaneous paintings and drawings

View of the Port of Swansea, 1729 (D/D Xgc)

Engravings of Glamorgan castles and churches by Samuel and Nathaniel Buck, 1740-1741 (unlisted); east view of Swansea, by Samuel and Nathaniel Buck, 1748 (CC/S Pl/X)

Drawings of Glamorgan by Emma and Lucy Bacon, 1827-1828 (D/D Xgb)

Aerial view of Swansea, 1885 (D/D X 192)

Watercolour of the Cenotaph, Swansea, 1922 (D10)

Engravings of views in the Swansea and Neath Valleys, various dates (D248)

North west view of Penrice Castle, by Samuel and Nathaniel Buck, 1741

FILMS

Mayor-making ceremonies, 1933-1993 (P/CF)

Swansea municipal films, *circa* 1936-1989, including grant of city status, 1969 (P/CF and P/VID)

Amateur films of Port Talbot, 1930s-1940s (D/D Z 278)

Steel Company of Wales publicity films, 1948, *circa* 1950 (D/D Z 278)

Aberavon Gasworks, *circa* 1959 (D/D Xlm)

SOUND RECORDINGS

Recordings of reminiscences of Swansea people, *circa* 1975-1980 (TH)

NEWSPAPERS

The Cambrian: accounts and miscellanea, 1786-1896; articles of association, 1890-1899; correspondence, 1851-1912 (SL WM)

The Cambrian Daily Leader: 1881-1890 (CDL)

Herald of Wales: 1932-1968 (Swansea edition, with a number of other editions including topical editions) (D6)

South Wales Evening Post: 1931-date (with gaps) (D6)

Advance notice is required to use the last two items. Local newspapers are also kept at the Swansea Reference Library, Alexandra Road. Most are available on microfilm and hence are easier to use. The Library also maintains an index to *The Cambrian*, which is a useful source for nineteenth century Swansea history.

Newscutting books

Newscutting books concerning events in Swansea, 1899-1937 (D/D Z 20)

First Day covers for newspapers celebrating Swansea's city status, 1969 (D254)

Newscutting books concerning events in Swansea, compiled by William John Cornish, n.d. (D262)

General

A history of the South Wales newspapers to 1855, 1954 (D/D Z 256)

RELATED RECORDS IN OTHER REPOSITORIES

National Library of Wales

The National Library of Wales, Aberystwyth, holds collections of national significance for Wales, and also many collections of local significance. Amongst the record collections which relate to the whole of Wales are diocesan records for all the Welsh dioceses, including most notably pre-1858 wills, and some parish records from all over the Principality. The National Library also holds estate records and personal papers, some of which directly relate to other records held by the West Glamorgan Archive Service. For instance, there are Penrice and Margam Estate records in both Swansea and Aberystwyth, so it is important for the reader interested in these particular estates to search the lists of both repositories. The other principal estate collections relating to West Glamorgan are the Badminton Collection (Beaufort Estate) and the Penllergaer Estate Collection.

Library of the University of Wales, Swansea

The Archive Section of the University Library, Singleton Park, Swansea, holds a number of collections which overlap with those held by the West Glamorgan Archive Service. The early Swansea Borough charters, Roman Catholic records for parishes in Swansea, various business, industrial and estate collections, all complement collections listed above.

Glamorgan Record Office, Cardiff

The Glamorgan Record Office at County Hall, Cathays Park, Cardiff, holds several collections which relate to the whole of the former county of Glamorgan. The principal such collections are those of the former Glamorgan County Council and of the Glamorgan Quarter Sessions. Others include pre-1948 South Wales colliery records, records of the Glamorgan Constabulary and those of the South Wales Monthly Meeting of the Society of Friends. The Cardiff Library Collection, now held by the Glamorgan Record Office, includes records relating to most of Wales and has a number of items relating to West Glamorgan, including early charters of the Borough of Neath.

INDEXES OF PERSONS
AND PLACES

INDEXES OF PERSONS AND PLACES

This guide is intended to be self-indexing by subject: the indexes below are provided for the benefit of users interested in particular persons or places.

INDEX OF PERSONS

INDEX OF PLACES

All places are in the historic County of Glamorgan unless otherwise specified. Other counties given are the pre-1974 counties.